The Capstone Handbook

Cory Lock, Editor

St. Edward's University

KENDALL/HUNT PUBLISHING COMPANY
4050 Westmark Drive   Dubuque, Iowa   52002

Acknowledgments

The <u>Capstone Handbook</u> results from the work of numerous authors, reviewers, and other contributors. The first version was written by William J. Zanardi in the early 1980s. This was edited and expanded by Catherine Rainwater in 1991 and again by Anna Skinner in 1992 and 1993.

A completely revised edition was written in 1997 by Susan Loughran, with the assistance of Catherine Rainwater, Virginia Dailey, Anne Crane I.H.M., and James Payne, among others. It was again updated in 2004 to include a chapter on the St. Edward's Moral Reasoning Across the Curriculum initiative. Danny Ursery provided particularly influential feedback for this chapter.

This most recent revision again reflects the input of many St. Edward's faculty members and former students. It draws extensively from the 2005 <u>New College Capstone Handbook</u>, which was edited by Joanne Sánchez and Jeff Trower and directed by a revision committee consisting of Sue Currey, Jennifer Greene, Joe O'Neal, Joanne Sánchez, and Jeff Trower. The <u>Capstone Handbook's</u> chapter on Library Research was revised by the library staff, and the MLA Format chapter was revised and considerably expanded by Bob Strong. Many Capstone instructors contributed course documents and other content; this revision directly relies on the work of Peter Beck, Ken Hamstra, Bunny Joubert, Susan Loughran, Michelle Moragne e Silva, Bob Strong, and Brett Westbrook. It also includes sample student writing sections drawn from the final Capstone papers of SEU alumni Paulette Garcia and Drew Watson.

During the revision process, Jack Green Musselman provided helpful input to the fallacy section, and Joanna Robinson gave detailed feedback on the handbook as a whole. Former Capstone Instructors of the Year Dianne Brownlee, Anne Crane, and Bob Strong and Capstone Director Susan Loughran gave generously of their time in reviewing the final manuscript. Professors Loughran and Strong were also of invaluable help throughout the summer-long revision process.

I would like to extend my sincere thanks to all the <u>Capstone Handbook</u> contributors.

Cory Lock
January 2007

Contents

Introduction

Welcome to the Capstone Course

As the capstone is the crowning point of any structure, so is this course considered the crowning achievement of your liberal arts education at St. Edward's University. Your semester-long project will provide you an opportunity to showcase the skills you have mastered during your college career. All of us on the Capstone faculty want you to succeed in the Capstone Course. We want you to end your years at St. Edward's with a feeling of pride in both the work you do in this course and the knowledge you have gained as a result of taking it. The standards are high, and we expect you to work diligently, but we anticipate that you will experience the pleasure of achievement as well.

The St. Edward's Mission Statement asks all of us to "confront the critical issues of society." The Capstone Course is directly related to that charge. In this course, you will be asked to study an individually selected social controversy. On one level, you will be required to discover where others stand in relation to the problem you are investigating. You will need to consider who is involved in the controversy, what issues dominate the debate, and what solutions and supporting arguments specific groups propose relating to these issues. You will also be required to explore the values and principles that underlie their positions.

Your thinking, however, must not stop at what others think about this social debate. It must extend beyond that level to analyze where *you* stand in relation to the controversy you have selected. As a liberally educated person, you know that the resolution of these kinds of social controversies will be in your hands in the future. St. Edward's graduates in particular should be prepared to recognize their responsibility to the world community and to find ways to make a difference in the world around them. The Capstone Course offers an opportunity for you to explore and analyze your own beliefs, assumptions, values, and goals, as well as those of others. It will help you to become the kind of critical thinker and problem solver that is needed to face the challenges of the twenty-first century.

Course Overview

The St. Edward's curriculum is designed to provide you with a balanced education, one that stresses critical and creative thinking, moral reasoning, problem solving, communicating, and assuming social responsibility. This began in the liberal studies section of the Freshman Studies Program where you reflected on your identity and your relation to the rest of society. This kind of work continued throughout your college career in the General Education classes. Now, near the end of your time at St. Edward's, the Capstone Course will help ensure that you are properly prepared to take an active role in shaping society and to handle the challenges of future decades.

Carrying out these tasks requires a variety of skills. By your final semesters of college these should be fairly well developed. You are already acquainted with research procedures for identifying reliable sources of information about public debates and their participants. You also have the ability to identify and analyze the arguments voiced in these debates and to uncover the value conflicts inherent in these controversies. Finally, you have acquired the written and oral communication skills needed to present research, arguments, and conclusions clearly and persuasively. Capstone is your opportunity to both hone and showcase all of these skills.

Course Requirements

Specific requirements for each Capstone Course section appear on the class syllabus. Although each instructor will adapt the information in this Handbook to some extent, the faculty will be fairly consistent in what they ask of students in the course. Briefly, the standard requirements are as follows:

- Selection of an appropriate topic that meets the course requirements
- A single paper on the chosen controversy, merged into a cohesive whole, including the following five stages:
    - Submission One—Foundational Research
    - Submission Two—Presentation of Library Research
    - Submission Three—Analysis and Evaluation of the Controversy
    - Submission Four—Experiential Component and Revised Solution
    - Submission Five—Final Revision
- One or more oral presentations on the selected topic
- A research file containing the work from all phases of the project
- Three or more personal interviews with the course instructor
- Two or more in-person interviews with experts on your topic
- A civic engagement activity in which you take a concrete action to support your final conclusion

In addition, a portion of your Capstone grade will depend on your participation throughout the semester. You must attend all scheduled class meetings and conferences with your instructor. Most instructors will not allow you to turn in papers that are late or incomplete. Instructors are also not obliged to reschedule missed interviews or read late papers. Under no circumstances can the final paper be turned in late. It is your responsibility to attend class and keep up with the syllabus.

The following is a useful set of guidelines to help you understand more specifically the kinds of tasks that you will need to accomplish as part of your Capstone project.

Research Tasks

- State the central research problem in the form of a precise and open normative question.
- Outline the major steps in the project design.
- Utilize technology to identify both library and online sources adequate in number and quality to the demands of the project.
- Evaluate the reliability of sources.
- Define key terms.
- Identify the limits of the research project.
- Present your research in a clear, thorough, and coherent manner.
- Interpret the research data; i.e., tell what they mean rather than simply reproducing them.
- Evaluate and attempt to resolve disagreements among the sources used.
- Locate and interview in person experts on your social controversy.

Presentation of Research Findings

- Clarify why a given research topic is worth investigating.
- Identify competing positions regarding a given controversy.

- Identify the parties involved in the controversy.
- Identify and clearly formulate the issues, arguments, and evidence involved in the research topic.
- Identify the plans made and actions taken by various parties in order to bring about their proposed solutions.
- Identify and analyze the values inherent in the controversy.

Critical Thinking and Moral Reasoning

- Use critical thinking to evaluate the strengths and weaknesses of the alternative positions.
- Use moral reasoning to analyze the ethical components of the alternative positions.
- Formulate a hypothesis relating to your own position on the controversy.
- Present a policy-based solution to the controversy.
- Indicate how that solution is warranted by logic or evidence.
- Argue persuasively for your hypothesis.
- Act in a concrete way on your hypothesis.

Communication Tasks

Written

- Compose complete sentences free of basic punctuation and spelling errors.
- Write unified and coherent paragraphs.
- Organize paragraphs in a logical, coherent sequence appropriate to the design of the project.
- Maintain a formal style appropriate to a scholarly audience.
- Revise in response to the evaluations of others.
- Employ standard Modern Language Association (MLA) documentation and bibliographical forms.

Oral

- Communicate appropriately in an interpersonal format during scheduled meetings with your instructor.
- Deal effectively with other students in a small group communication format.
- Employ effective interview techniques.
- Revise your project according to feedback from your interviewees.
- Give at least one formal oral presentation, adhering to standard communication techniques in both form and content.

Research File

One of the requirements of this course is that you maintain an organized research file throughout all phases of your Capstone project. Your instructor may examine this file at any time throughout the semester. It will be turned in at the end of the semester at the same time you submit your final paper. Your instructor will keep it until the deadline for grade appeals has passed. After that time, it will be returned to you if you have notified your instructor in advance that you would like it returned and you reclaim it at the agreed-upon time. Otherwise, your instructor will destroy it.

Goals

There are several reasons for preparing this file.

- It will provide a place to keep the material you are collecting.
- It will help you keep that material organized.
- It will provide a record of the thoroughness with which you have prepared and carried out your research.
- It will document your work in case there is any question about it.

What to Keep

Basically you are required to keep *everything* pertaining to this project in your file:

- Class notes
- Prewriting (such as topic ideas, research ideas, etc.)
- Preliminary bibliography
- Photocopied articles and book chapters
- Printouts of World Wide Web material
- Notes on all books, articles, etc., used in the project
- Graded copies of your papers
- Comment and grading sheets prepared by the instructor
- Names, addresses, and phone numbers of interviewees
- Field research notes (and tapes if used)
- All drafts (not just copies of the submitted papers), including drafts shown to or commented on by ANY Writing Center or private tutors
  Save all the phases of your writing before you make changes. Put all of these documents (both handwritten and printed-out) in your research file; they are your only proof that you have composed the paper as required.

NOTE

In addition to saving all written material related to your Capstone project, remember to save your electronic work as well. If you have not already done so, get in the habit of *regularly* backing up the work on your computer. Also, save your work to *multiple* locations (such as hard drive, EdShare, USB drive, and/or disk).

Check with your instructor regarding what type of file you should use for your Capstone project. Some instructors require accordion folders, while others may allow ring binders, accordion folders, index card files, and various combinations of these.

NAME _____   ID #: _____

E-MAIL: _____   PHONE: _____

MAJOR: _____   MINOR: _____

Are you planning on graduating this semester?   Y   N

Is there anything about which you think I should know that might affect your concentration and time available this semester? Activities you may want to list include participation on a sports team or in a performance, a heavy course load, a heavy work schedule, or participation in any other time-consuming project.

Do you have any disabilities that I need to accommodate in this course?   Y   N

If yes, are you registered with Academic Planning and Support?   Y   N

If yes, do you have a 504 letter?   Y   N

Please explain below the accommodations you will need, or speak to me personally after class.

OPTIONAL: Do you have any other concerns about your ability to succeed in this course that you would like to share with me? Such concerns might include being a nonnative speaker of English; difficulties in a past American Dilemmas, Capstone, or writing course; or general anxieties about the organization, writing, and research required for this course. Include only the concerns you feel like sharing.

TO REVIEW

You are being asked to choose and study a social controversy; consider others' positions; and ultimately propose, explain, and argue for a particular solution. You will use research, argumentation, critical thinking, moral reasoning, and communication skills in your work. You will be asked to complete a unified research paper in five stages: the foundational research stage, the presentation of your library research, the analysis and evaluation of your library research, the experiential component and presentation of a fully supported solution, and the polished final paper. Throughout the semester you will be meeting individually with your instructor to discuss your work and communicating with your peers, then making revisions as a result of those interactions. In addition, you will be keeping a file that records all the work you have been doing on the project. Finally, at least once during the semester, you will orally present the results of your research project to the class in a formal presentation.

Components of the Capstone Course

The Topic Proposal

Capstone Topic Requirements

The first step in a successful Capstone project is choosing your topic. All Capstone topics need to involve a current social controversy. Many of you are in "open topics" sections. That means that as long as your topic conforms to the following requirements and is approved by your instructor, it may involve most social controversies. Others are in sections with a topical heading, which limits your choices of social controversies. For example, if the generic topic of your section is "Education Issues," your Capstone project needs to focus on a controversy that involves children in some way. You could investigate a question such as "Should for-profit companies run publicly funded schools?" If you are unsure about your type of Capstone section, ask your instructor.

Since the world is a complex place, continuously embroiled in conflict, a diverse range of topics is available for your Capstone project. However, you must meet a number of criteria to fulfill the parameters of analysis.

Your Capstone Topic Must Be . . .

- a *current* social controversy.
- presented as an open-ended normative question and not already formulated as a conclusion.
- an issue with identifiable value conflicts.
- open to a potential solution that could be implemented as policy by entities such as private corporations or government agencies.
- narrow enough to allow adequate treatment in the time available.
- one for which sufficient written, scholarly materials are available.
- one that offers local opportunities for in-person interviews with experts on your particular controversy.
- of high personal interest to sustain your concentration and energy for the duration of the course.
- one that allows you the opportunity to take a concrete action to inform or support your conclusion (e.g., attending a meeting or rally, circulating a petition, volunteering).
- one about which you have not made up your mind, so that you can look fairly at all sides of the question.
- one that is not on your instructor's list of prohibited topics, if he or she has presented you with such a list.

NOTE

If you are planning to investigate the same topic you used for another major research paper, you must first obtain the permission of your instructor. If your topic is approved, you will be required to provide a copy of the previous paper. YOU CANNOT USE YOUR AMERICAN DILEMMAS TOPIC (OR ANY WORK FROM THAT PAPER) FOR YOUR CAPSTONE PROJECT.

What Are "Identifiable Value Conflicts"?

Values are ideals that people strive toward, and it is through value identification and understanding that we are able to clarify the conflicts that drive controversial issues in the first place. In the process, various solutions are offered as a means of resolving those dilemmas.

For example, suppose you would like to focus on genetics. One question about genetics is "What is recombinant DNA research?" While this is an engaging and timely subject, it does not involve a value-laden dilemma. Instead, the question merely prompts a descriptive study of the field and, therefore, would not be a suitable Capstone topic. A better question in that same area of interest might be "Should agricultural genetic engineering be subject to federal regulations?" This dilemma pits scientific advancement and the resultant benefits of genetic engineering against the concerns of consumers and a nonscientific community; it also pits federal responsibility for maintaining public safety against the practice of unfettered scientific research and free enterprise.

What Is an "Open-Ended Question"?

If your research question is a suitable one, then your current stance on the issue can be influenced; that is, you are open to listening to more than one side of the controversy and are willing to explore alternate possible solutions. A "closed" question reveals that you have already formed an opinion. It is therefore inappropriate for a Capstone topic since it would result in a very one-sided and subjective final paper. An example of this type of biased questioning is "Why is it wrong for insurance companies to have access to genetic information on policyholders?" The word *wrong* automatically implies that you, the writer, have made up your mind and that you have not examined the controversy sufficiently to determine such a policy's strengths. An acceptable rewording of a similar question on the same topic would read, "Should insurance companies have access to genetic information on policyholders?"

Another example of a research question that manifests bias is, "How can citizens prevent the construction of nuclear power plants?" While nuclear power plants might have their fair share of adversaries, the question implies that nuclear power plants are inherently dangerous and that their construction should be prevented at all costs. A viable research question would be more along the lines of "Should the United States government allow construction of additional nuclear power plants as an alternate energy source?" An unbiased question such as this not only allows for discussion of alternate energy sources but also presents a balanced analysis of both the advantages and disadvantages of using nuclear energy.

Remember that the same principle of balanced objectivity applies to your selection of research materials. Obviously, you should not limit your sources to materials provided by only one party of the controversy and certainly not to sources that address only one side of the issue. This demonstrates an inability or unwillingness on your part to look squarely at both sides. Rather, you must use a variety of reputable sources that reflects the opinions and arguments of all the major parties.

Tips for Choosing a Topic

In choosing your topic, consider whether a policy will emerge from the way your research question is answered. For example, "How should serious juvenile offenders be punished?" will give rise to different policies depending on how it is answered. "Why has the juvenile crime rate increased in recent years?" will not.

Test your tentative ideas to make sure they are appropriate by analyzing the moral component to the controversy. Ask yourself, "Why is this topic worth studying?" and "What values or ideals do the parties in the controversy appeal to in arguing their positions?" A successful Capstone paper must address such a conflict over values.

Finding and Defining a Topic

Each instructor will have somewhat different requirements for this stage of your research. The following information, however, provides some helpful pointers:

- Start compiling a list of possible Capstone topics in your research notebook. Consider controversial topics that you have read about or have seen in the media. Try to recall any questions or discussions that may have emerged in other classes that lend themselves to further exploration. In particular, you may want to investigate controversies related to your major or other areas of personal interest.

- Narrow your list to two or three possible topics, preferably those that will challenge any preconceived notions you may already have. Identify the one you find most intriguing, provided that it has two or more debatable sides.

- Formulate that controversial issue as precisely as possible into an appropriate normative, or "should," question. As you do so, consider whether a policy will emerge from the way it is answered. For example, the question "Should juvenile offenders who have committed serious crimes be punished or rehabilitated?" will allow for the rise of different policies depending on how it is answered. However, something like "Why has the juvenile crime rate increased in recent years?" will not yield policy or action. This is nothing more than a declarative statement reconfigured as a question.

Evaluating Your Topic

It is essential that you test your topic idea to make sure it is appropriate by asking the following questions: Why is this topic worth studying? What is its significance to me personally and to society in general? To what values do the parties in conflict appeal in arguing their positions? In other words, what claims are the parties making, and what are the values and supporting premises in those claims?

While many phenomena involve legitimate and interesting questions, keep in mind that some simply do not inspire debates with at least two credible sides to the controversy. Such subjects might include the existence of child abuse, senseless murders, the reemergence of Nazism, the proliferation of hate crimes, the destruction of the ozone layer, and the use of nuclear weapons—volatile subjects in their own right but difficult to make arguments "for." As an objective researcher, you would be hard-pressed to find legitimate arguments supporting subject areas like these.

What you might find, however, embedded in each of these subjects are questions that could be developed into viable Capstone topics, subjects that are equally illustrative of some controversy previously unacknowledged and unexplored. The rise of neo-Nazism, for example, might be a manifestation of inner city class struggles or of socioeconomic conditions in which neo-Nazi parties take up hatred and scapegoating as a means of self-defense from the brutality of joblessness, hunger, and ignorance. Dealing with the rise of neo-Nazism and its sources would most likely involve oppositional parties offering differing policies to alleviate this social problem, thus allowing for an intriguing Capstone topic. The same shift in focus toward policy holds true for the other subjects mentioned previously: how to deal with adults who abuse children, how to deal with those who commit hate crimes against homosexuals, how to monitor the effects of global warming, how to monitor the proliferation of nuclear stockpiles in North Korea. Most topics that involve conflict, and that could result in public policy for the betterment of society, are appropriate for your Capstone project.

REMEMBER!

Keep in mind that your topic must be current; it must be controversial; it must be open to debate from two or more sides; and it must have room for a potential and legitimate solution that could result in policy. Be sure to state the central research problem in the form of a precise "should" question, and contact your instructor to discuss your topic idea and to get final approval.

Possible Capstone Paper Topics

What follows is a sampling of viable Capstone topics formulated into appropriate "should" questions. These questions are provided as examples for you to use in finding a unique Capstone question that engages your own personal interests. In order to find a topic that will motivate you for the entire semester, do not simply pull a "ready-made" research question from the following list, but instead use them as models in formulating an appropriate question related to a controversy that interests *you*.

- Should for-profit companies run publicly funded schools?
- Should the off-shoring of jobs be subject to government oversight and regulation?
- Should employers implement mandatory drug testing in the workplace?
- Should juvenile offenders be tried and incarcerated as adults?
- Should religion and character education be taught in public schools?
- Should prescription drugs be available over the Internet?
- Should employee e-mail be accessible to employer scrutiny?
- Should the United States adopt English as its official language?
- Should insurance companies have access to genetic information on policyholders?
- Should the United States mandate the use of a national ID card?
- Should local governments implement sex offender notification laws?
- Should green-card military enlistments be encouraged as a means for attaining American citizenship?
- Should the United States undertake a manned mission to Mars?

Class Activity: Capstone Topic Identification

Determine which topic questions in the following list are suitable for a Capstone project. If you judge a topic to be unsuitable, explain why, based on the previous section on "Choosing Your Topic: Capstone Paper Requirements."

1. What are the effects of embryonic stem cell research?
2. Should the use of cell phones be prohibited while a person is driving?
3. Why is it wrong to decriminalize drugs?
4. Is global warming detrimental to human existence?
5. Should children who commit violent crimes be treated as adults in the criminal justice system?
6. Has the federal government diminished the rights of U.S. citizens since 9/11?
7. Should chimpanzees continue to be exploited as test subjects for the sake of science?
8. Should racial profiling be used as a tool in the war on terrorism?
9. Should the burning of the American flag be made unconstitutional?
10. Should the United States really spend upwards of $1 trillion on an expedition to Mars?
11. Should the Internet be regulated?
12. Should Botswana charge fees for state education?

Class Activity: Capstone Topic Collaboration

Participate in a small-group discussion of an issue that has a strong and controversial moral dimension. Your instructor may assign your group a social problem or may encourage your group to identify your own.

STEP 1

Identify a controversial social problem (or, alternatively, your instructor may assign your group a social problem to investigate). At this point, do not worry about policies. Instead, try to identify something that is wrong with society and needs to be fixed. Examples: teen pregnancy, corporate fraud, unemployment, etc.

SAMPLE GROUP RESPONSE:
teen pregnancy

STEP 2

Make a list of controversial topics that surround your social problem.

SAMPLE GROUP RESPONSE:
sex education
religion/character education
birth control
resources for pregnant teens
parental notification requirements for abortions

STEP 3

Choose three of the topics you listed in Step 2. For each of these topics, identify at least one controversial policy that relates to it. Keep in mind that one topic may involve multiple controversial social policies. For example, the topic of resources for pregnant teens could involve teen pregnancy helplines, programs providing financial support for teen mothers, in-school day care for the children of teen mothers, etc. As you identify the social policy, be sure to make it clear what entity (government agency, corporation, nonprofit organization, etc.) would be responsible for administering the policy.

SAMPLE GROUP RESPONSE:
sex education: abstinence-only education programs in U.S. public schools
birth control: distribution of free condoms in all Austin Independent School District high schools
parental notification: requirement by the state of Texas of notification of both parents of women under 18 seeking abortions

STEP 4

Working from the policies you listed in Step 3, formulate three potential Capstone questions. As you do so, remember to maintain a neutral tone.

SAMPLE GROUP RESPONSE:

Should the federal government fund abstinence-only sex education programs in public schools?

Should AISD distribute free condoms at all its high schools?

Should the state of Texas require the notification of both parents (or guardians) of women under 18 years old seeking an abortion?

STEP 5

Select a member of your group to report the results of your work to the rest of the class.

Though instructors' policies for topic submission may vary slightly, you will need to obtain your instructor's approval for your Capstone topic before proceeding to Submission One. Remember, if you would like to pursue a topic on which you have already written another major research paper, *you must first obtain your instructor's consent*. YOU CANNOT USE THE SAME TOPIC FOR YOUR CAPSTONE PROJECT AS YOU DID FOR AMERICAN DILEMMAS.

WHEN YOU FINISH SELECTING A TOPIC, YOU WILL HAVE CARRIED OUT THIS CAPSTONE COURSE TASK:

- State the central research problem in the form of a precise and open question.

Submission One: Foundational Research

After your topic is approved by your instructor, the next step in your Capstone Course project is to begin your research. The goal of Submission One is to show your grasp of the terminology you will be using throughout this semester, particularly by applying it to your own topic, and to demonstrate there are enough sources of sufficient variety to sustain your project. The assignment is in two parts, requiring you both to complete the Topic Analysis Form and to produce an annotated bibliography. Naturally, as you write your paper and continue your research, you may have to revise the major components of your project that you identify in Submission One. However, the concepts and sources you identify here will serve as a guide for your work throughout the semester.

At the end of this section, you will find a suggested Topic Analysis Form and Annotated Bibliography Instructions. Your instructor may use these instructions or alternatively may provide you with his or her own version of them. All Submission One assignments will require you to understand the vocabulary that follows, apply this vocabulary to your own project, and identify and evaluate a number of scholarly sources relevant to your project. For more on locating and assessing sources, see the "Library Research" section of this handbook.

Capstone Vocabulary

Social Problem

All Capstone projects deal with competing approaches to bettering something that is wrong with society. This wrong is the social problem. While your Capstone project may address one primary social problem, it will most likely address more than one. For example, a controversy over building more jails in Texas may concern the social problems of both jail overcrowding and crime. The debate surrounding lowering an area's highway speed limit from 65 to 55 might address the social problems of both high rates of traffic accident fatalities and air pollution. Identifying and documenting a clear and urgent social problem is essential to your Capstone project because this establishes why the controversy you are investigating—and thus your entire paper—is important and worthy of your readers' attention.

Proposed Solution/Policy Option

For the purposes of the Capstone Course, a proposed solution is one group of people's plan for fixing a social problem. For example, building jails is a proposed solution to jail overcrowding and crime. Lowering the speed limit is a proposed solution to excessive highway accidents and air pollution. Some instructors may also call the proposed solution a *policy option* because this emphasizes the fact that all proposed solutions investigated for the Capstone Course must be concrete policies that can be enacted by a government agency, corporation, nonprofit, or other agency. Solutions that simply propose a change in attitude (e.g., littering less, reducing carbon dioxide emissions) without targeting a specific policy are unacceptable for this project.

Topic Question

This is the question that will serve as the unifying focus of your paper. It will be the title of your Capstone paper, and you will include it at the end of your opening paragraph(s) in the location where you may be accustomed to placing a thesis statement. The Capstone paper begins with a topic question, rather than a thesis statement, because much of the project involves neutrally investigating the controversy rather than arguing an assertion throughout the paper, as you may have been accustomed to do for other assignments. The topic question must reflect the controversy over a proposed solution to a specific social problem. Thus, it is a normative question, in that it describes a debate over what society *should* or *should not* do. For more on selecting and articulating a topic question, see the previous "Choosing Your Topic" section.

Sides

Because your project investigates a controversy, you will need to identify and examine at least two sides. Sides are basically the groups of people unified by a shared answer to the topic question. At the least, there are two sides to any controversy—one opposing a proposed policy and one supporting it. However, do not limit yourself to two sides. There may be a third or even a fourth. For example, in the question "Should abortion remain legal?" you may find a side that is against abortion in any case, a side that is for abortion, and a third side that is for abortion only in limited circumstances. For purposes of efficiency, you may want to give each side a nickname or label. Examples of such nicknames include:

> Opponents and proponents of [a particular policy]
>
> Side A and Side B
>
> Environmentalists and developers
>
> Liberals, conservatives, and moderates

Position

A position is one side's answer to the topic question. It implies a particular stance. For example, in response to the topic question "Should the state of Texas institute a school voucher program?" you might identify Side A's position supporting the implementation of a voucher program and Side B's position against the voucher program.

Parties (General and Specific)

A side is by no means a homogeneous group of people. Instead, it consists of numerous parties, or stakeholders, who may differ otherwise but are unified by their position within the controversy. These groups often have different reasons for their support but may end up on the same side. For example, both feminists and religious fundamentalists oppose pornography, but for different reasons. Further, some groups of people may be split on an issue. For example, in the debate over regulating the prescription of antidepressants to adolescents, psychiatrists and parents of depressed children fall on both sides of the issue.

As you discuss the groups who make up each side of a controversy, you will need to distinguish between general and specific parties. General parties are broad types of people who have taken a specific position. Yet keep in mind it is rare that any single group will be purely of one mind on any controversy. In particular, you will likely find members of the same professional groups on both sides of the issue. Therefore, the use of qualifiers in discussing general parties is extremely important. For example, suppose your question is "Should the United States government endorse surrogate motherhood?" You have identified one position as those who argue that a woman's right to control her body as a financially rewarding surrogate service amounts to child selling, leading to the exploitation of women. You might find that the general parties of lawyers, physicians, theologians, and parents involved in this issue articulate essentially the same point of view, albeit from diverse backgrounds. Yet, it is possible that research might reveal that some lawyers, some physicians, some theologians, and some adoptive parents are of the pro-surrogate persuasion. In order to accurately describe the general parties to the debate, you will need to qualify as specifically as possible what portion of the party supports each position. Rather than say the general parties of the anti-surrogate side are physicians and parents, it might be more accurate to say "some physicians and many parents." Even better, you may have encountered even more specific data in your research. If so, use it! You could say, "A 2006 survey by researchers at the Stanford University revealed 72% of parents of school-age children oppose surrogate motherhood when it involves financial compensation."

Sample Qualifiers

Some
Most
Many
All
A few
Half
72% of

Specific parties are those leading the charge for a particular side. They may be named groups or individuals. Keep in mind that neither the courts, which interpret the law, nor governmental agencies, which enforce the law, are parties in a controversy. Organizations that make up the specific parties to a debate might include Planned Parenthood, The Sierra Club, Greenpeace, Centers for Disease Control, the National Institute of Health, the National Association for the Advancement of Colored People, the American Civil Liberties Union, The Salk Institute, Persons for the Ethical Treatment of Animals, Microsoft, and the National Aeronautic and Space Administration.

Individual parties should be identified according to titles, affiliations, or honors. Individuals acting as specific parties might include Michael Dell, Chairman of the Board; California Congresswoman and Speaker of the House Nancy Pelosi; Sandra Froman, President of the National Rifle Association; and Michael DeBakey, world-renowned physician and heart surgeon. As you can see, the possibilities for identifying specific entities and individuals are virtually unlimited. The important thing to remember is that professional titles establish credibility, both for you and your sources.

NOTE

Be sure the titles you attribute to individual parties are current! Keep in mind that a person who held a particular position at the time of your source's publication may no longer do so.

Issues and Arguments

Issues are the broad concerns over which the sides are arguing. Most instructors will require you to identify at least three issues within your controversy, yet many of you will identify four to five. Generally, the various sides to the debate will concern themselves with the same issues, though they will approach and prioritize them differently. For example, in a controversy such as "Should water quality standards be more stringent in Austin?" cost is an issue about which all groups, both pro and con, will be concerned. Each side will have developed arguments that relate to the issue of cost.

Arguments support each side's position on a particular issue. In the previous example, the anti-stringency perspective may argue that "Increased regulations will cost too much for the benefits they may bring." The other side might argue, "No matter the cost of increased regulations, they are worth it if they improve water quality and thus increase safety." Effective arguments are composed of claims backed up with supporting reasons. They should be evaluated both for their internal logic and for the quality and quantity of evidence that supports them. For more on identifying and analyzing arguments, see the "Argumentation" section of this handbook.

Evidence

Evidence is what each side uses to back up its arguments. In Submission Two you will be presenting the evidence each side uses to make its case. This can include statistical information, precedents, case studies, and expert testimony. In Submission Three you will be evaluating this evidence according to quantity and quality. Therefore, even as you begin your research, it is important for you to start identifying each side's evidence. For more on evidence see the "Argumentation" section of this handbook.

Plans/Actions

Each side is doing more than simply making arguments to support its positions. Both sides are also making plans and taking actions to ensure their position is the one in force. The plans and actions you identify should be practical and concrete. The parties of each side may be carrying them out now, or the parties may be planning to undertake them at an identifiable point in the future. Examples of plans and actions include developing proposals, creating media campaigns, lobbying, carrying out grassroots efforts, and working with the electoral system at various levels.

Values

Values are beliefs about what is good and desirable or what is undesirable and to be avoided. Examples include justice, privacy, beauty, health, safety, honesty, tolerance, creativity, and rationality. Values are not usually identified in the statements of debating parties. They are usually implicitly, rather than explicitly, stated. Therefore, you will have to infer the values that are being advocated from the case presented by each side. Each position is supported by a number of values. Sometimes sides may hold values that are in contradiction with each other, while in other cases sides may share values but approach or prioritize them differently.

Though most of your discussion of values and moral reasoning will not come until Submission Three, it is important that you start attending to values early in your project. This is because values are the foundation, the underlying cause, of each side's position on a controversy. They are, in essence, what the sides are debating. For example, in the debate over making English the official national language, proponents value national pride, security, and fiscal savings (resulting from government agencies not being required to provide translators, multilingual documents, etc.). Opponents value diversity, equal opportunities for immigrants, and tolerance. Both sides might be said to value cultural tradition, but proponents emphasize our nation's Anglo heritage, while opponents celebrate and attempt to preserve the multiple cultures that have made the United States what it is. Each side's arguments will be founded on these values, based on beliefs regarding what ultimately is best for the American nation.

Class Activity: Understanding the Capstone Vocabulary

Your goal for this activity is to complete a sample Topic Analysis Form in a group of three or four other students.

1. Your instructor will likely assign your group a topic. If not, your group should begin by selecting one that fits the guidelines listed in the previous section, "Capstone Topic Requirements."

2. Using either a copy of the Topic Analysis Form (your instructor will likely ask you to use the form included in this handbook for Submission One) or a separate piece of paper, complete all the form's questions as a group. Refer to the previous "Capstone Vocabulary" section for help understanding the terminology.

3. After all the groups have completed the form, share your results with the class. As you do so, explain any specific difficulties or insights your group had in completing the exercise.

Optional Instructions
Submission One: Annotated Bibliography

In this assignment you will produce an annotated bibliography that will help you begin the process of scrutinizing your sources for credibility. The purpose is to make sure that there are enough credible sources of sufficient variety to sustain your Capstone project. For this part of Submission One you will need to do two things:

1. Find 14 authoritative sources, 7 for each side, according to the instructions below.

NOTE

Eventually you will need at least 25 credible written sources and two field interview sources.

---

2. Annotate your sources, according to the instructions below.

Authoritative Sources

For Submission One, you need to locate 14 sources, 7 for each side. For **each side,** you will need:

- 1 book or book chapter
- 1 scholarly journal article or authoritative newspaper article
- 1 credible web site
- 3 additional authoritative sources (book or book chapter, scholarly journal, authoritative newspaper article, credible web site, government document, or report/document from relevant organization)
- 1 possible interview subject

REMEMBER

You are looking for a variety of solid authoritative (credible) sources, not just the first source you find that relates to your topic.

NOTE

You may find a strong neutral source, covering multiple sides of the issue, that you want to use. Ask your instructor if such a source is permissible and, if so, how to include it in your bibliography.

Books or Book Chapters

Books give you an overview of your controversy and are often the best way to begin the research process. These must be books by a single author, not a collection of essays put together by an editor. They must be intended for a professional or well-educated lay audience (children's books and high school textbooks are not acceptable).

NOTE

The SEU library keeps several reference sources on current social issues, such as <u>Opposing Viewpoints</u>, which is an edited collection of essays. These do not meet the standards required for the kind of primary research required in Capstone. They are not acceptable for this assignment or for use at all in your Capstone project. Ask if you are not sure something is acceptable.

Scholarly Journal Articles

Journal articles will be more narrowly focused than books, and they often give you more current information on your controversy. Journal articles that are acceptable for this assignment are written for a specific audience, as opposed to a general audience. In addition, they are peer-reviewed. Authors must have significant credentials to be considered experts in the field (you will need to determine this). You may retrieve these articles from online sources, such as databases, if they are full text. Abstracts are not acceptable for this assignment or for use at all in your Capstone project.

Newspaper Articles

Information about some topics is more likely to be found in newspapers than in scholarly journals. When using a newspaper, use the most credible and respected publication possible. For general topics this might include newspapers such as the <u>New York Times</u> or the <u>Washington Post</u>. If you are working on a local topic, newspapers such as the <u>Austin American-Statesman</u> and the <u>Austin Chronicle</u> will be important sources.

Web Sites

Web sites can be a valuable source of research information, but they have to be carefully evaluated. Web sites used for this assignment must have been recently updated with clear authorship and responsibility for content. Generally, the web sites of government agencies, accredited academic institutions, and credible organizations (such as the NAACP or the AMA) are considered acceptable. Wikipedia is not an acceptable site, as it does not meet the above standards.

Other Written Sources

For the Submission One assignment, these are limited to:

- Government documents
- Reports, pamphlets or other material gathered from relevant organizations

Interview Subjects

Your interview subjects must be real, local people you can interview later in the semester. You do NOT have to have interviewed the person by the time of the bibliography assignment. You do need to have located them to the extent of finding their name and contact information. Interview subjects must have educational, employment, or other significant experiential background in their area of expertise. It's best if they have contributed in an original way within the controversy you are investigating, such as through research, program design, or activism.

Annotation

Writing an annotated bibliography requires you to:

- Develop a standard MLA citation for each entry
- Summarize each source and discuss why it is a credible source and how it will contribute to your project
- Assemble your citations like the standard MLA Works Cited list, i.e., in alphabetical order according to author or the first major word in the title if there is no author

For more information on formatting your annotated bibliography, see Lesley University's "MLA Format for Annotated Bibliographies" at http://www.lesley.edu/library/guides/citation/mla_annotated.html

Grading

Your grade will be based on:

- Following instructions and meeting all requirements
- Quality of sources
- Quality of your annotations
- Accuracy of citations in the Works Cited list

Optional Instructions
Submission One
Topic Analysis

NOTE

You must have your topic approved before beginning work on Submission One. To complete Submission One, you must complete this form and attach to it an annotated bibliography. Refer to the Capstone Handbook and your notes from class for definitions of terms.

Keep in mind that the information you provide on this worksheet is just a start! You will be expected to revise and expand the information you include here as you continue your research.

I. General Information on Your Controversy

Identify at least one *social problem* relevant to your controversy:

Provide two statistics and/or forms of evidence demonstrating the extent or seriousness of the stated social problem. Provide citations for each statistic that reference a work or works on your attached annotated bibliography.

1)

2)

Identify three different *solutions or policy options* that have been proposed to address the social problem:

1)

2)

3)

State the *topic question* (one of the possible solutions framed as a normative question). Hint: begin sentence with *should*.

II. Side 1

Identify this side's *position* (in other words, its answer to the topic question):

General parties to the controversy (general types of people who have a vested interest in the controversy; be sure to include qualifiers as appropriate):

1)

2)

3)

Specific parties to the controversy (particular groups or individuals spearheading this side's actions; be sure to include titles and qualifications of individuals):

1)

2)

3)

Issues (name at least three broad concerns the sides are debating):

1)

2)

3)

4)

5)

Arguments relating to these issues.
List a major argument Side 1 makes relating to issue #1:

List a major argument Side 1 makes relating to issue #2:

List a major argument Side 1 makes relating to issue #3:

List a major argument Side 1 makes relating to issue #4 (if you have identified an issue #4):

List a major argument Side 1 makes relating to issue #5 (if you have identified an issue #5):

Plans/Actions (What are this side's parties doing to ensure that their position is the one in force?):

1)

2)

Values (What values underlie the arguments used?):

1)

2)

3)

III. Side 2

Identify this side's *position* (in other words, its answer to the topic question):

General parties to the controversy (general types of people who have a vested interest in the controversy; be sure to include qualifiers as appropriate):

1)

2)

3)

Specific parties to the controversy (particular groups or individuals spearheading this side's actions; be sure to include titles and qualifications of individuals):

1)

2)

3)

Issues (name at least three broad concerns the sides are debating):

1)

2)

3)

4)

5)

Arguments relating to these issues.
List a major argument Side 2 makes relating to issue #1:

List a major argument Side 2 makes relating to issue #2:

List a major argument Side 2 makes relating to issue #3:

List a major argument Side 2 makes relating to issue #4 (if you have identified an issue #4):

List a major argument Side 2 makes relating to issue #5 (if you have identified an issue #5):

Plans/Actions (What are this side's parties doing to ensure that their position is the one in force?):

1)

2)

Values (What values underlie the arguments used?):

1)

2)

3)

WHEN YOU FINISH SUBMISSION ONE, YOU WILL HAVE CARRIED OUT THESE CAPSTONE COURSE TASKS:

- Outline the major steps in the project design.

- Utilize technology to identify both library and online sources adequate in number and quality to the demands of the project.

- Evaluate the reliability of sources.

- Identify competing positions regarding a given controversy.

- Identify the parties involved in the controversy.

- Identify and clearly formulate the issues, arguments, and evidence involved in the research topic.

- Identify the plans made and actions taken by various parties to bring about their proposed solutions.

- Identify the values inherent in the controversy.

Submission Two: Presentation of Library Research

Purpose and Organization of Submission Two

In Submission One you completed a series of exercises designed to help you ensure there are sufficient scholarly sources available for your Capstone paper and identify the major components of the debate you are investigating. By the time you complete Submission Two, you should have completed the bulk of your library research. In this phase you will begin writing your Capstone paper by introducing the reader to your project and clearly presenting the major components of the controversy, based upon the information you have gained through your research.

Each instructor will use slightly different criteria, but the format on the following pages will give you an idea of what is expected for Submission Two. In general, Submission Two will be about fourteen to twenty pages in length and will use approximately twenty-five credible sources. It should begin with a title that states your topic question and an introduction that acquaints the reader with the topic. Other initial components include a discussion of the social problem(s) your controversy addresses, definitions of relevant terminology, a brief discussion of secondary issues, and a statement of the scope of your project. The main body of the paper should be a combination of historical narrative and objective presentation of the controversy backed by extensive research.

You may find that you will need to modify your "should" question, for in each successive stage of your research and writing, you will learn more about your issue. Throughout the composition of Submission Two, you must remain neutral and avoid using any emotional and biased language. You should support a stance in Submission Three only after objectively considering all aspects of the controversy presented in Submission Two.

Introduction

Begin by writing an interesting opening paragraph (or two if necessary) that acquaints your reader with the research topic. Your research question should appear at the end of this introduction. Keep in mind that your research question, which also serves as the title of your paper, will dictate the overall direction of your paper. Be careful to state it as clearly and precisely as possible for this stage of your work. Whatever is established up front must be followed through in the rest of your Capstone paper.

Documentation of Social Problem(s)

In this crucial section of your paper, you identify the significance of the topic. Why should the reader be concerned about the controversy you have selected? What is the inherent conflict that makes this topic controversial? In particular, how is the controversy likely to affect your reader and other members of society? Keep in mind that this section establishes the groundwork for your reader's interest in this topic in the first place. In answering these questions, you should *document at least one social problem* that the parties to your controversy are attempting to solve, albeit in different ways. Although the two opposing sides will most likely have completely different interpretations of the social problem(s), it is your job to remain objective and analytical. In showing the social problem(s) are real and pressing, you should provide relevant statistics and other evidence to back up the claims you make. If your project has a personal significance, you may also want to mention it here.

Definitions

Each topic will have special terminology you need to identify and define to help the reader gain a clear understanding of the debate. Conceptual definitions are beneficial in setting the parameters for discussion. Let us assume, for example, that your topic question is, "Should the government regulate the use of electroconvulsive therapy (ECT) on psychiatric patients?" It is important that you explain how you will use certain complex terms in your paper. For example, you will need to define *government*; does that mean federal, state, or local government? Also, what is the precise definition of ECT? How does it work? If current laws are to be changed, what exactly are those laws? The type of psychiatric patient would also need to be stipulated, which may mean identifying and defining types of psychiatric disorders that might be treated with ECT, as well as identifying the varying levels of severity of the disorder. Most psychiatric disorders are fully defined in the <u>Diagnostic and Statistical Manual for Psychiatry</u>; therefore, you would need to identify that source as the standard in diagnosing psychiatric disorders. You would also need to define any specialized terminology, technical language, or abbreviations with which the reader may be unfamiliar. Subsequent definitions may be woven into the body of the paper.

Secondary Issues and Scope

Because the Capstone project is narrow and deep, rather than broad, in scope, secondary issues naturally arise from the various positions you are researching. If there are secondary issues that are worthy of mention but that you will not focus on in your paper, mention them here. Secondary issues may involve who the decision makers are, who the beneficiaries are, and who incurs liability. One way to think of secondary issues is to imagine them as orbiting the primary issue, your chosen topic. While their significance may be relevant, their importance is still subordinate to that of the parent issue. For example, in a project on stem cell research, which involves considering whether the destruction of a fertilized egg is morally reprehensible, the effect such arguments could have on the abortion controversy would be a secondary issue. Undoubtedly, this section will be augmented and revised before submitting the final paper.

Describing your project's scope consists of explaining to the reader the limitations, depth, and breadth of topic as well as what precisely you intend to cover. You will also need to explain why you are placing these limitations on your research. For example, you have chosen the topic "Should corporal punishment be applied in American schools?" During your research you have discovered that the nature of private schools, where parents can remove their children if they are uncomfortable with the discipline policies, is very different from that of public schools, which are supported by American tax dollars, open to everyone, and the only schooling option available for most Americans. Therefore, you decide to limit the scope of your research to public schools only. Specificity of this nature is crucial in establishing and maintaining the overall scope and direction of your paper. As you can see, your thesis question and scope are intricately linked.

Background on the Controversy

Next you will need to transition into a history of your topic. While this section should generally be organized chronologically, it is not simply a list of important dates. Instead, you should *narrate*, explaining what events happened and why they were significant. This section should be a history of the *controversy* more than a history of the issue itself. For example, a project investigating if corporations should monitor employee e-mail would provide background on when this practice began and on other forms of corporate surveillance of employees. It would *not* give a detailed history of e-mail in the workplace.

Depending on the subject, the temporal span of the historical narrative will vary from one student paper to another. If your topic involves e-mail surveillance, your history section might focus primarily on events of the past twenty years. However, if your topic deals with juveniles being tried and incarcerated as adults, your history may extend as far back as a few hundred years, in which case you will summarize the highlights as succinctly as possible before narrating the controversy's more immediate history.

No matter what their temporal scope, all papers should explain the origins of the controversy and bring the reader up to date on recent events. In essence, the history section provides whatever background information the reader requires to understand the current situation. Yet, remember that the Capstone Course is not primarily a history project. Give enough information to put the problems you are investigating in context, but no more. Generally two to four pages are sufficient. You may wish to address the following questions as a checklist for thoroughness:

- Where, when, and how did the controversy originate?
- Who were the initial parties to the controversy?
- How has the controversy developed over time?
- What are the most significant milestones in terms of laws, events, court cases, and changing social conditions?
- What is the current state of the controversy?

Presentation of Cases

In this section you lay out the heart of the debate as informed by your research. In presenting the cases, you will need to use the same terminology you dealt with in completing your Topic Analysis Form for Submission One. Therefore, you should review the definitions provided in the previous section of this handbook before beginning. However, while Submission One touched on the concepts of positions, specific and general parties, issues, arguments, and plans briefly and in outline form, in Submission Two you will much more thoroughly explain how these concepts play out within your controversy. Additionally, you will be adding an emphasis on *evidence,* explaining how each side supports its arguments. In presenting such a detailed synopsis of your controversy, you will be relying heavily on library research, including both the sources you identified in Submission One and new scholarly sources you have since discovered. The following provides details on the specifics of what should be covered in your presentation of cases.

Positions, Parties, and Sides to the Controversy

You will need to begin this section by clearly identifying at least two positions to the controversy you are investigating. Remember, another way to think of this is as identifying the various major responses to your thesis question. If your question is "Should the federal government fund research projects using new lines of embryonic stem cells?" you might focus on two positions: those who answer "yes" to the question and those who respond "no." Yet you might also choose to organize your paper by highlighting three possible positions: the previous two plus those who argue "yes" the government should fund some new lines of stem cells but who insist on particular regulations regarding the sources of those lines. For many positions you identify, you will need to begin the Presentation of Cases section of your paper by clearly identifying the major sides to the debate and the positions associated with them.

Once you have identified the major sides and positions, you will next need to explain exactly who is participating in the debate by discussing the general and specific parties. Identifying both the general and the specific parties involved or likely to be affected by the controversy adds dimension and credibility to your paper; therefore, you must provide the names of these groups and individuals. Also provide any specifics that add to the credibility of the group or individual, such as job titles or relevant honors. As you discuss parties, be sure to be as specific as possible, using qualifiers as discussed in the "Capstone Vocabulary" section of this handbook under "Parties."

Issues, Arguments, and Evidence

After identifying each side's overreaching position and the parties who make up each side, you are ready to move on to discussing the issues each side is arguing, the specific arguments each side makes about those issues, and finally the evidence the sides use to support their claims. As you do so, you will be expanding on the points you touched on in your Topic Analysis Form but explaining them in more detail and adding a discussion of evidence.

As an example, in a project entitled "Should health care workers be tested for HIV?" the Submission One Topic Analysis Form would mention that one of the issues in contention is cost. It would also note with no elaboration that those opposed argue that the cost of testing all workers would be prohibitive, while those in favor contend that if even one life is saved, any cost is worth paying.

In Submission Two the issue of cost would likewise be addressed, but in a much more detailed fashion. Statistics, studies, scholarly analysis, and other support for each side would need to be included. The goal here is to give whatever evidence you as the researcher can find that each side uses to support its arguments related to the issue of cost. Be sure to review the "Argumentation" section for more information on recognizing and understanding arguments and evidence.

Plans/Actions

Finally, in presenting the cases you will need to identify each side's plans. What is each side doing to ensure that its position is adopted? Look for concrete actions the sides are planning or currently carrying out.

Transition

Conclude your presentation of the cases in Submission Two by highlighting what is most important about the information you have just presented. You should additionally provide a transition to Submission Three, in which you will evaluate the argumentation and moral reasoning of each side to the controversy. Your instructor may also ask you to identify the primary value conflicts within the controversy at this point as a way of emphasizing the ethical components of the conflict as you move from presenting information to analyzing it.

Appendix Format and Content

Many instructors may also require you to submit at least one appendix with Submission Two. The purpose of appendices is to provide your reader with the concrete details of laws, regulations, and other information pertinent to your controversy. Appendices generally contain information that is too long for you to quote within your paper, but which your reader may want to reference, such as charts, laws, and maps. All appendices should appear *before* the Works Cited list and should be included in the consecutive page numbering of your paper. However, they do not count toward the required page length total. At the top of the page, centered, type Appendix A (or B, C, etc.). Follow this a line below with a subtitle that indicates the content of the appendix. Example:

Appendix A

Texas Penal Code, Title 5: Offenses Against the Person

Chapter 19. Criminal Homicide. . .

Remember, your appendices are a part of your paper *and should be formatted as such.* Xerox copies or printouts from other sources are not acceptable. Be sure to include only what material is pertinent to your controversy. For example, for a paper on capital punishment in Texas, you would likely only need to include Section 19.03 of the Texas Penal Code, which deals with capital murder—not all of Chapter 19, which deals with all different types of criminal homicide.

Works Cited

Submission Two and all subsequent submissions must be accompanied with a Works Cited list in accurate MLA format that lists all sources (whether paraphrased or quoted) you have used in creating your paper. See the "MLA Format" section of this handbook or the <u>MLA Handbook</u> for more on using and accurately citing outside sources.

Class Activity: Identifying Capstone Vocabulary

Your instructor will specify whether to carry out the following activity individually or in groups.

1. Read the article entitled "Should the Draft Be Reinstated?". Your instructor will provide you with a copy of the article.

2. Drawing from the article, indicate the major positions and corresponding sides within the controversy over reinstating the draft.

3. Next, for each side you have listed, identify:
   - General parties
   - Specific parties
   - Issues
   - Arguments
   - Plans/Actions
   - Values

Optional Instructions
Submission Two
Peer Review Guidelines

Respond to the following questions as thoroughly as possible on a separate sheet of paper. Be sure to include both your name (as the reviewer) and your partner's name (as the writer) on your responses. Feel free to write on your partner's draft wherever necessary, but do not let these comments replace the detailed, comprehensive comments that the peer review requires.

Basic Format

Check if your partner's paper is in the proper format. See "MLA Style Basics" in the Capstone Handbook's chapter on MLA Style for specific guidelines.

Does it have a header on the upper right hand corner of every page that includes the author's last name and the page number? Does the paper include your partner's name, instructor's name, course name and section, and the date in the upper left corner of the first page? Does the paper begin with a title that is the writer's Capstone question?

Introduction, Documentation of Social Problem, Definitions, and Scope

Does the introductory section contain the components in the following list? What, if anything is missing? What, if anything, needs to be expanded or revised? Any suggestions on how to do so?

- Introductory paragraph(s), ending with research question *Yes*
- Documentation of social problem, including relevant statistics *Yes*
- Definitions *Yes*
- Secondary issues and scope *Yes*

History and Background

1. Do you completely understand the background to this controversy? Or, do certain past events or developments still need to be elaborated? Is the history section up to date? Does it acquaint the reader with events up to the present time? Explain.
2. Is this section arranged chronologically? Is it easy to follow? Explain.

Presentation of Cases

1. Does your partner specifically identify positions, parties (general *and* specific), issues, arguments, evidence, and plans? If not, be sure to indicate what is missing.
2. Does your partner thoroughly address each of the previous components? Identify any areas that need expansion or revision.
3. If you have not done so already, analyze your partner's presentation of cases. *Does it make sense?* Is he/she missing something important?

39

s Cited

Are there at least twenty-five sources? Do the sources used substantially add to the content of the paper? Do they support *both* positions? Does the writer use a range of *scholarly* sources, such as books and journals? Are any other sources used, such as magazines and newspaper articles, Web sites, and government publications, credible and appropriate to this scholarly project? Basically, when you look at this paper, do you say, "Wow! My partner did a lot of research"? Or are the sources merely adequate? If this is the case, what types of sources might your partner add?

Organization

1. Are the paragraphs of your partner's paper ordered in a logical manner? Does the order of the paper's major points make sense? Explain.
2. Are the points your partner makes *within* each paragraph organized? Does each paragraph have a topic sentence that sums up all the points that follow? Do the sentences within each paragraph all relate to each other? Does your partner use transitions to show the relationship between points? Explain.

Grammar, Spelling, and Punctuation

Mark whatever errors you encountered on the draft itself. Then, indicate here any errors your partner appears to be repeating. Consider misspelled words, run-on sentences, problems with pronoun agreement, and other grammatical rules.

MLA Form

Are the paper's parenthetical citations and Works Cited list in proper MLA format? If you're not sure, consult the "MLA Format" section of the Capstone Handbook or the MLA Handbook. Mark what appears to be incorrect.

Style and Tone

1. Does your partner's paper seem completely neutral? Or, can you tell which way he/she is leaning? Please mark any sections that sound biased.
2. Does the overall tone seem clear and coherent? Any problems with wordiness? Any places where the writer seems too informal? Any other style or tone issues? Explain.

Final Comments

Any final suggestions or words of encouragement? This is a good place to tell the writer what he/she did well. At the very least, answer the following question: *How did reading your partner's draft influence your perception of your own Capstone paper?*

WHEN YOU FINISH SUBMISSION TWO, YOU WILL HAVE CARRIED OUT ALL THE PREVIOUS CAPSTONE COURSE TASKS, AS WELL AS:

- Clarify why a given topic is worth investigating.

- Define key terms.

- Identify the limits of the research project.

- Present your research in a clear, thorough, and coherent manner.

- Interpret the research data; i.e., tell what they mean rather than simply reproducing them.

- Evaluate and attempt to resolve disagreements among the sources used.

- Compose complete sentences free of basic punctuation and spelling errors.

- Write unified and coherent paragraphs.

- Organize paragraphs in a logical, coherent sequence appropriate to the design of the project.

- Maintain a formal style appropriate to a scholarly audience.

- Employ standard MLA documentation and bibliographical forms.

Submission Three: Analysis and Evaluation of the Controversy

The first portion of Submission Three is composed of Submission Two, which should be thoroughly revised and lengthened according to comments, suggestions, and concerns raised by your instructor and classmates (if your class uses peer review). Consider visiting the SEU Writing Center for help with this revision process. See the "Composing a Research Paper" section of this handbook for more on the Writing Center and on using tutors at all stages of your Capstone project.

In the new content of Submission Three, you will analyze and evaluate both the critical thinking and the moral reasoning of each side. In doing this, your goal is to maintain the professional tone you began in Submission Two. Evaluate the strengths and weaknesses of each position, as well as each side's moral perspectives, using neutral, unbiased language. Finally, once you have fully presented and analyzed the cases as objectively as possible, you will be ready to present your own tentative solution. Submission Three will end with your tentative answer to the topic question, including your support or rejection of a specific policy and a presentation of the reasons behind your stance. Your paper at this point should be approximately nineteen to twenty-five pages long and use approximately twenty-five appropriate sources.

Critical Thinking: Analysis and Evaluation of Argumentation

A vitally important component of your Capstone Course project is your analysis of the material you have been researching. This is the point in the project where you present your own thoughts, rather than reporting on the ideas of others. The goal here is to answer the question "Which side has presented a stronger case and why?" In answering this question, you will need to review the cases presented by each side and analyze them point by point.

NOTE

In completing this section, you will need to carefully read "Section 3: Argumentation" of this handbook. It will give you objective criteria to use when evaluating the strengths and weaknesses of each side's arguments and evidence.

Below is a sample Analysis and Evaluation of Critical Thinking section drawn from a past student paper. It addresses the normative question: "Should Pregnant Drug Users Be Prosecuted for Fetal Abuse in the United States?" Though the structure and content of each Capstone paper will differ slightly, this selection provides an example for you to keep in mind when structuring your own analysis.

Having completed the presentation of the cases for both Side A and Side B, this writer will

proceed to analyze each issue to determine the strengths and weaknesses of each side's argu-

ments. On the issue of health and safety regarding prosecution, Side A maintains that prosecu-

tion will frighten pregnant drug users out of seeking needed medical treatment, while Side B says

that prosecution would promote treatment among pregnant drug users. Side A has a stronger case, partly due to the 120-interview study of former pregnant drug users that they cite. Side B referenced numerous medical facts from credible sources such as The National Association for Perinatal Addiction Research and Education to support its stance that prosecution is needed to maintain health for pregnant drug users and their infants. Yet, the interviews directly affirmed Side A's notion that prosecution prevents pregnant drug users from seeking out medical and drug treatment. Also, Side A's argument is far more realistic and logical. It is quite sensible to assume that a pregnant drug user will avoid seeking out treatment if she knows there is a possibility that she could be prosecuted for her actions. On the contrary, it is not very sensible to assume that the threat of prosecution will scare pregnant women out of using drugs. After all, society is still filled with drug abusers, even though the threat of prosecution lies behind drug abuse.

In regard to fairness, Side A claims that prosecution is a discriminatory, unfair solution to the controversy, but Side B reasons that prosecution is a fair solution. Side A also has a stronger case for this issue. This is due to the fact that Side B does not have enough substantive information to sustain its assertion that prosecution is not unfair or biased. Side A based its argument on multiple, professional past studies by groups such as the American Medical Association that imply the discriminatory nature of prosecution for pregnant drug abusers. On the other hand, the single statistic from Side B appears rather flimsy when compared to the numerous statistics utilized by Side A. Also, it is difficult for this writer to believe Side B's notion that prosecution is not biased against poor, minority women when one takes into account the way these women are popularly depicted as drug abusers by the mass media. To this writer, the picture of poor, minority women as drug users is so prominent in our society that it justifies why such women would be targeted by prosecutors.

Concerning the rights of pregnant women, Side A says the rights of pregnant women should not be infringed upon, even in cases of prenatal drug abuse. In contrast, Side B says the rights of pregnant women should be forfeited as necessary to protect the health of fetuses. Side B has a stronger case than Side A. Both sides referred to a single judiciary ruling for support, but Side B's position was more sympathetic to the health of infants. Conversely, Side A put more emphasis on feminist ideals. In the opinion of this writer, the rights of pregnant women are not ignored in cases of prenatal drug abuse, as Side A implies. Instead, these rights are prioritized behind infant health. For this writer, infant health takes precedence over feminist views regarding the rights of pregnant women.

On the final issue of fetal rights, Side A opposes fetal rights and prosecution, while Side B argues that the validity of fetal rights rationalizes prosecution. In this instance, Side B has a stronger argument. Side B provides sound evidence by specifically addressing medical and legal changes that treat fetuses as persons in the United States, while Side A gives vague reasons that fail to adequately dispute the idea that a fetus should be regarded as a child. Consequently, this writer views Side B's evidence in this argument regarding fetal rights as more substantive and convincing than Side A's evidence. Also, since fetal rights has been such a popular, controversial issue in our society due to the ongoing debate over abortion, this writer believes Side A could have provided more specific, persuasive evidence for its argument.

Moral Reasoning: Analysis and Evaluation of Ethical Perspectives

Following your discussion of the logic and evidence the various parties to your controversy present in support of their positions, you will need to discuss the ethical components of the controversy. This is yet another crucial section to your paper because value conflicts are at the heart of all Capstone controversies. While people debating whether or not parents should be allowed to withhold medical treatment for their children due to religious reasons may put forward logical reasoning and concrete evidence in support of their case, for many the controversy is most importantly about the less tangible values of personal responsibility, individual freedom, and the safety and health (both physical and mental) of children. In other words, the ethical component of the controversy may be as—or even more—important to the parties involved as the logic and evidence.

> ### NOTE
> "Section 4: Moral Reasoning" of this handbook deals exclusively with this subject and provides detailed instructions regarding the ethical analysis you should provide in this section of your paper.

The following is a sample analysis and evaluation of moral reasoning section drawn from the same student paper as excerpted previously.

In order to thoroughly evaluate the controversy over prenatal drug use, the moral reasoning of each side needs to be considered. Since proponents of rehabilitation focus on the well being and rights of the pregnant drug users, their primary obligation is to the pregnant drug users. This obligation is an informal obligation, resembling that of citizenship. Drug treatment proponents are also obligated to the women's unborn children, but they emphasize that prosecution will only frighten drug users away from seeking help, thus damaging more fetuses in the long run.

Since rehabilitation supporters favor drug treatment for pregnant drug users as opposed to prosecution, it is clear they value public health, particularly the health of pregnant women. Their concern with the prosecution being discriminatory and selective among various demographics of pregnant women shows this side's emphasis on fairness and equality. Finally, the concern of supporters of rehabilitation for the rights of pregnant women demonstrates their value of human rights. As determined by this writer, the most important of these values to the position are public health and fairness, which are repeatedly emphasized in their argumentation.

The consequences of rehabilitation supporters' solution to the controversy, which is the creation of more drug treatment programs for pregnant drug users, could have either positive or negative outcomes. If this solution succeeds, more treatment would be available for the pregnant drug abusers and the quality of infant health would improve in the United States. Of course, these outcomes would be beneficial, but long-range. Drug treatment programs could provide both physical and emotional benefits for both pregnant drug users and their infants, but it would take much time for these programs to be established and for the overall quality of infant health to improve in the country. If the solution fails, a great amount of money will have been wasted on new drug treatment programs and the quality of infant health in the United States will not improve. These outcomes would be both detrimental and long-range, since it would take years to prove that the new drug treatment programs failed to improve the quality of infant health in this country.

Finally, the normative principle used by treatment proponents seems to be the Principle of Rule Utilitarianism, which supports policies that help the greatest number of people possible over the long term. In relation to this principle, this side favors drug treatment programs over prosecution because this solution would produce good for both the mother and the fetus, as opposed to only the fetus. They emphasize Rule Utilitarianism, rather than Act Utilitarianism, in emphasizing the long-term benefits of policies that emphasize treatment over prosecution.

Due to prosecution supporters' great concern for how pregnant drug users can best care for their fetuses, their primary obligation is to the infants. Their main concern is ensuring the health of as many infants as possible. Yet, they also acknowledge an obligation to the mothers and believe that prosecution is the best way to make these women seek treatment. Finally, this side is obligated to the good of society as a whole, in their insistence that physical health of pregnant women is a public concern because the children they bear are the nation's future. Like those who support rehabilitation, prosecution supporters' obligations are also informal.

Given that this side views prosecution as a way of promoting health among both pregnant women and their fetuses, it is obvious that they value public health and child safety. In addition, prosecution proponents' strong support for fetal rights implies that they value justice and fairness. Thus, their values are embedded within their convictions.

The consequences of jail time for pregnant drug offenders could be either positive or negative. On one hand, this solution could be successful and cause prenatal drug use to decline in the United States. This outcome would be beneficial, but long-range. Specifically, it might take years for a positive trend to develop among pregnant women that would lower the number of pregnant drug users in the country. On the other hand, the solution of prosecution could prompt pregnant drug users to avoid medical treatment, which would have drastic effects on the health of the women and the infants. Of course, this outcome would be detrimental, especially to the physical well-being of pregnant drug users and their infants. Also, this outcome would be long-range, since it would take some time for a more negative trend to form among pregnant drug users in regard to their neglecting medical treatment.

All in all, this writer feels that the normative principle supporting the prosecution position is the Conventionalist Principle. This principle justifies punishing an act that is not in compliance and conformity with the rules and conventions of society. Accordingly, this side holds that it is morally permissible to prosecute pregnant drug users for risking the lives of their fetuses. Those in favor of jail time also follow the foundational normative Principle of Least Harm. Clearly, neither the option of prosecuting pregnant women and risking alienating them from seeking help nor that of failing to prosecute them and risking their continuing to use drugs is entirely positive. Yet, prosecution supporters suggest that this solution has the least potential for harm in that it more actively seeks an end to the women's drug abuse, which harms both the mother and the child.

Tentative Solution

This final section of Submission Three should follow logically from your analysis of the controversy. In it you should identify which position you support, the reasons for your position, *and what policy-based solution you recommend at this stage in your work.* In this final section of Submission Three, present the basics of your own proposal and the major arguments and moral reasoning that you feel support it in one or two paragraphs. Here you should directly answer your topic question, and you should show how the concrete policy you support will address the social problem(s) you began documenting at the beginning of your paper. For example, in a project investigating "Should the mentally handicapped be executed in Texas?" you could respond:

> After considering the argumentation and moral reasoning of both sides in the debate, I am against executing the mentally retarded. BRIEFLY SUMMARIZE THE ARGUMENTATION AND MORAL REASONING YOU FOUND MOST PERSUASIVE.

> To address the social problem of high violent crime rates in Texas, as well as to ensure justice for victims and their families, I propose a two-part solution: stronger sentencing guidelines regarding life sentencing and giving juries the option to sentence perpetrators to life without parole. BRIEFLY EXPLAIN HOW YOUR SOLUTION WOULD ADDRESS THE SOCIAL PROBLEM (I.E., WHY IT WILL WORK).

In presenting your tentative solution, you should directly address the major strengths and weaknesses of the other side's argument; in other words, you should construct a counterargument. For example, imagine that your paper is entitled "Should Texas School Districts Adopt Year-Round Schooling?" You are supporting the status quo rather than a change to a new system. You might respond to the arguments and evidence of those proposing year-round schooling with the following counterargument:

> Those in favor of year-round schooling argue that it will save taxpayers money. They give some credible statistics to support their position, and this writer is not disputing the estimated savings. However, no amount of money saved is worth the potential damage to the families involved. Year-round schooling will make it almost impossible for individual family members to schedule family activities and vacations together.

You will also want to respond to important ethical objections of your opponents, as in the following counterargument example involving the controversy over the death penalty:

> Proponents argue that there are few abuses because of the stringent guidelines involving the death penalty. I believe that any abuse—even one innocent person killed unjustly—is too much. The potential safety of society must not be prioritized over one individual's human rights.

At this point, it is also appropriate to discuss any reservations or doubts you have about your tentative solution and to mention issues you may want to investigate further when you conduct your interviews. Some instructors may give you the option of participating in your civic engagement activity at this stage in your project. If this is the case in your section, you may consider presenting your civic engagement activity here as another way of getting information on your tentative solution. If you do, be sure to review "Civic Engagement" in the following section on Submission Four.

Remember, the tentative solution you present here is not your revised solution. It is one that you will investigate further during the interviews you conduct in Submission Four. It is also not your final defense of your conclusion; this will be added at the end of Submission Four as the conclusion of your entire paper.

Optional Instructions
Submission Three
Peer Review Guidelines

Respond to the following questions as thoroughly as possible on a separate sheet of paper. Be sure to include both your name (as the reviewer) and your partner's name (as the writer) on your responses. Feel free to write on your partner's draft wherever necessary, but do not let these comments replace the detailed, comprehensive comments that the peer review requires.

Basic Format

Check if your partner's paper is in the proper format. Does it have a header on the upper right hand corner of every page that includes the author's last name and the page number? Does the paper include your partner's name, instructor's name, course name and section, and the date in the upper left corner of the first page? Does the paper begin with a title that is the writer's Capstone question?

Submission Two Revision

If your instructor has asked you to read the Submission Two portion of your partner's paper, answer the following questions. If not, move on to the next section.

Does the introductory section contain the components in the following list? What, if anything is missing? What, if anything, needs to be expanded or revised? Any suggestions on how to do so?

- Introductory paragraph(s), ending with research question
- Documentation of social problem, including relevant statistics
- Definitions
- Secondary issues and scope

Do you feel like you completely understand the background to this controversy? Or, do certain past events or developments still need to be explained? Explain.

Does your partner specifically identify and thoroughly address positions, parties (general *and* specific), issues, arguments, evidence, and plans? Identify any areas that need expansion or revision.

Has the writer successfully revised Submission Two so that it smoothly transitions to the new material? Or, do some parts seem choppy or out of place? Explain.

Critical Thinking Analysis and Evaluation

In this section, does your partner do all of the following?

1. Clearly present the issues being debated by the various positions? Analyze the strengths and weaknesses of each side's arguments? Explain.
2. Convincingly assess which side has the strongest overall logic and evidence?

Moral Reasoning Analysis and Evaluation

In this section, does your partner do all of the following?

1. Discuss each side's obligations?
2. Discuss each side's values?

3. Discuss the consequences of each side's position?

4. Discuss the normative principles that support each side?

5. Convincingly assess which side has the strongest overall ethical argument?

Be sure to explain your responses, rather than simply providing yes or no answers.

Tentative Solution

Does your partner briefly present his/her tentative solution *and* the reasons behind it? Does the solution involve a concrete *policy*? Is it clear how such a solution will address the social problem(s) identified earlier in the paper?

If you partner has chosen to discuss his/her civic engagement activity at this point, does it seem meaningful and relevant?

Works Cited

Are there at least twenty-five sources? Do the sources used substantially add to the content of the paper? Do they support *both* positions? Does the writer use a range of *scholarly* sources, such as books and journals? Are any other sources used, such as magazines and newspaper articles, Web sites, and government publications, credible and appropriate to this scholarly project? Basically, when you look at this paper, do you say "Wow! My partner did a lot of research"? Or are the sources merely adequate? If this is the case, what types of sources might your partner add?

Organization

Are the paragraphs of your partner's paper ordered in a logical manner? Does the order of the paper's major points make sense? Explain.

Are the points your partner makes *within* each paragraph organized? Does each paragraph have a topic sentence that sums up all the points that follow? Do the sentences within each paragraph all relate to each other? Does your partner use transitions to show the relationship between points? Explain.

Grammar, Spelling, and Punctuation

Mark whatever errors you encountered on the draft itself. Then, indicate here any errors your partner appears to be repeating. Consider misspelled words, run-on sentences, problems with pronoun agreement, and other grammatical rules.

MLA Form

Are the paper's parenthetical citations and Works Cited list in proper MLA format? If you're not sure, consult the "MLA Format" section of your Capstone handbook or the <u>MLA Handbook</u>. Mark what appears to be incorrect.

Style and Tone

Does the overall tone seem clear and coherent? Any problems with wordiness? Any places where the writer seems too informal? Any other style or tone issues? Explain.

Final Comments

Any final suggestions or words of encouragement? This is a good place to tell the writer what he/she did well. At the very least, answer the following question: *How did reading your partner's draft influence your perception of your own Capstone paper?*

**WHEN YOU FINISH SUBMISSION THREE,
YOU WILL HAVE CARRIED OUT ALL OF THE PREVIOUS
CAPSTONE COURSE TASKS, AS WELL AS:**

- Use critical thinking to evaluate the strengths and weaknesses of the alternative positions.

- Use moral reasoning to analyze the ethical components of the alternative positions.

- Formulate a hypothesis relating to your own position on the controversy.

- Present a policy-based solution to the controversy.

- Revise in response to the evaluations of others.

Submission Four: Experiential Component and Revised Solution

As part of your Capstone Course project, you will be required to do research in the field—the "real-world" environment of your controversy. This work will involve several steps:

- Identifying experts

- Designing an interview questionnaire

- Interviewing

- Writing up the results of your field research

- Analyzing the information you have received

- Formulating and arguing for a solution to the controversy

- Taking concrete action on your conclusion

In Submission Four your Capstone paper will take its final form; you may only need to revise it for accuracy, style, and grammar in Submission Five. Submission Four, like the final paper, should be approximately twenty-three to thirty pages long and use approximately twenty-five credible sources. Your instructor may specify a minimum or maximum page length, so be sure your paper fits his or her individual guidelines.

Expert Interviews

Gathering information from real people directly involved in your controversy is an important adjunct to your library research. It should enable you to:

- Develop your communications skills

- View your controversy from a somewhat different perspective

- Gather more information about your topic

- Get reactions to the tentative conclusion you developed in Submission Three

Expert Interview Requirements

All Capstone projects must fulfill the following interview requirements. Your instructor may, however, require additional components.

You must interview at least two people. These required interviews must meet the following criteria:

- Face-to-face: In other words, they cannot be conducted by telephone or e-mail.

- Diverse interview perspectives: your interview subjects should represent *different* sides of your controversy.

- Non-SEU interview subjects: One of the goals of this component of your Capstone project is for you to practice identifying resources and interacting with professionals outside the university community. Therefore, except in rare circumstances, Saint Edward's faculty, staff, and students cannot be used for the two required interviews.

- No relatives: For the same reason, your parents, aunts, uncles, grandparents, and other relatives do not qualify.

- Documented and easy to contact: You must provide your instructor with the name, title, address, and telephone number of each of your interview subjects. For reasons of confidentiality, the address and telephone number of your interview subjects should not be included within your Capstone paper itself, but should be instead submitted within your research file or directly to your instructor (as he or she indicates).

Your instructor may require additional interviews. He or she may also permit interviews that do not meet these requirements *if they are in excess of the two required.*

Identifying Experts

Before you even begin searching for interview subjects, make sure you understand the requirements. Once you have made sure your prospective subjects meet these requirements, you should keep in mind the following tips as you begin deciding whom to contact for an interview:

- Choose interviewees who have some expertise in the area of the problem you are studying. Realize that strong opinions do not necessarily make someone an expert. For example, having experienced corporal punishment does not make one an expert on the subject. Expertise usually comes with work and/or educational experiences.

- Before the interview, find out whatever you can about the interviewee's position as it relates to your controversy and the position of the organization he or she represents (if applicable). This will help ensure your interviewees represent different sides of the controversy.

- The individuals you interview should be located in the Austin area—or at least an area you are prepared to visit in person to conduct the interview.

Some students struggle with finding interview subjects who meet all the requirements. In order to ensure you successfully complete your interviews in time to analyze them for Submission Four, consider the following search techniques.

- Begin looking for and contacting possible interviewees *as early as possible.* Keep in mind that it usually takes several weeks to find appropriate people and arrange an interview.

- Try multiple sources for locating appropriate people. Don't give up if some initial Web searches do not prove productive. The reference librarians and faculty members at St. Edward's, as well as the telephone directory and information offices in local schools, businesses, unions, or associations, are good sources for recommendations about possible interviewees.

- Try multiple ways of contacting people. If an e-mail message does not yield a response, try the telephone. If telephone calls are not working either, try in-person visits to the offices of appropriate organizations.

- Rather than attempting to contact subjects one at a time, cast a wide net. Keeping in mind that not all subjects will turn out to be appropriate or available, try contacting two to three times as many people as you are required to interview.

- Setting up an interview may take several phone calls back and forth. Make sure you have a phone number where the prospective interviewee can leave a message, and make sure your answering machine or cell phone message presents you as a credible interviewer.

- If you are not available during regular business hours, it may be more efficient for you to find out if there is a good time to reach your prospective interviewee and call back.

- Remember that even if a person does not work out as an interview subject, he or she can still be a valuable source of information. Ask for suggestions of other names and organizations. If the person is a useful subject, but is unavailable for an interview, ask if he or she might be willing to answer questions by e-mail or telephone. This will not count toward your two in-person interviews, but may yield useful supplemental information.

Designing an Interview Questionnaire

Designing a good questionnaire is essential to conducting a successful interview. Your goal is to create clear, unbiased questions that encourage your interview subjects to discuss their perspectives. To meet this goal, keep the following tips in mind:

- Avoid asking for information that is available to you by other means. For example, read an organization's Web site before interviewing one of its members. You may find biographical information, including qualifications of your interview subject, and you may also find details of the organization's position on the controversy. This will make it unnecessary to ask questions like "What are your credentials?" or "What do you know about my controversy?" at the interview.

- Base your questions on the social problem to be solved and on information (such as the major issues, arguments, and values) that you reported in Submission Two and analyzed in Submission Three of your project.

- Make sure the questions are focused, specific, and substantial. They should elicit discussion rather than a "yes" or "no" response. Every question should contain probes (Why? How?) that will encourage discussion. Rather than "Do you favor increased regulation of Ritalin prescriptions for children?" ask "Where do you stand on the issue of safety regarding the widespread prescription of Ritalin to children?"

- Create unbiased questions. Bias may be subtle, yet noticeable to your interview subjects, so take care in constructing your questionnaire. For example, avoid leading questions such as "Shouldn't the federal government adopt a flat tax system?" A more neutral way to frame the same question is, "Do you consider the flat tax system to be equitable to all social classes?" Be careful that the terminology you use likewise does not suggest bias. For example, the words used to describe the sides in the abortion debate are themselves hotly contested. While those opposed to abortion might refer to the other side as "anti-life" and those supporting a woman's right to choose might refer to their opponents as "anti-choice," these terms are highly charged. Avoid them, instead referring to each side by what they call themselves, "pro-choice" and "pro-life" or by the even more neutral "supporters of legalized abortion" and "abortion opponents."

- Develop the questions in a logical sequence.

- Plan to ask five to eight questions.

- Be sure to ask all your interview subjects about your proposed solution. This will give you practical feedback on the critical thinking and moral reasoning that has led you to your solution and on the feasibility of the solution itself.

- Get your questionnaire approved by your instructor before you begin your interviews.

A copy of your interview questions should be included in the final paper as an appendix. See the "Submission Two" section of this handbook for specifics on formatting the appendix.

Preparing for the Interview

The people you will be interviewing for your project are doing you a favor in meeting with you. Keeping this in mind, you should handle this aspect of the project in an especially professional manner. Careful preparation will help you do this.

- Prepare in advance what you are going to say when you approach each interviewee. Be able to briefly describe the Capstone Course in general terms as well as your specific controversy.

- Decide what sort of note taking or recording equipment you will use before the interview. If you choose to audio- or video-tape the interview, practice using the equipment in advance. Make sure you have a battery-operated machine with charged batteries and several long-playing tapes. Avoid fussing with the recorder during the interview.

NOTE

Taped interviews require advanced written permission of the subject. It is best to ask your subjects for permission to tape *as you set up the initial interview.* Then, when you meet for the interview, obtain written consent before you begin taping.

- Even if you plan to tape the interview, be sure to bring up a notebook and writing utensil as a backup in case your subject declines being taped.

- Gather as much background information as you can on your interview subjects and the organizations with which they are affiliated.

- If you are nervous about or inexperienced at interviewing, consider practicing with a friend or, at least, reading the questions out loud.

Conducting the Interview

Conducting a successful interview takes skill. The goal is to establish a friendly, professional environment that will encourage the interviewee to respond to your questions. Remember: you asked for the interview, so it is your responsibility to conduct it. Here are some tips to help you succeed.

- Be on time.

- Dress appropriately.

- If you plan to tape the interview, ask in advance if you can do so—preferably as you are initially setting up the interview. Then, obtain written permission from the interview subject before you begin taping.

- Consider starting the interview with a concise summary of your work to date.

- Listen—do not talk. You asked for the interviews to hear what your experts have to say, not to impress them with your knowledge. Ask for clarification if you need it, but be aware that interrupting every few sentences will become annoying.

- Do not be afraid to deviate from your questionnaire if that seems appropriate; however, make sure that the interview stays on track and does not ramble off the topic.

- Be objective and open-minded even if you disagree with the respondent. Remember, you are gathering information, not debating.

- Remain courteous at all times.

- Ask your respondents to recommend resource material. Professionals usually know about excellent information that you may not have found in your library research.

Again, these professionals are doing you a favor. At the least, a follow-up thank-you note or e-mail after the interview is required. Use professional-looking stationery and make sure the letters or e-mails are neat and literate. You may want to send a copy of your finished project or even volunteer some time to work with the individuals or groups you have consulted. If an interviewee has requested a copy of your paper, you are obligated to provide a copy to him/her. Overall, thanking your interviewee for his or her time and effort will help present you and St. Edward's University in the best light possible. And, remember, many Capstone students have made useful professional contacts during the interview process!

Writing Up the Results of Your Field Research

Write up each interview as soon as you get home, even if you have it on tape. Your memory will fade if you do not, and you are then more likely to misrepresent your source.

Begin with a smooth and interesting transition into this portion of the paper. One approach is to move from the discussion of your tentative solution to an introduction of your interviewees. In the following example, the writer presents her tentative conclusion:

Thus far, this writer is inclined to support the position of treatment for pregnant drug users for three reasons. First, the arguments for this position were more convincing than those for jailing such offenders. Second, the potential negative outcomes for treatment programs are not as detrimental as jailing's possible negative consequence. In other words, this writer does not view the loss of money to be as serious as a decline in public health, namely that of newborns. And finally, this writer believes that the implementation of drug programs for pregnant drug users is the best method for lowering the percentage of prenatal drug abuse in the United States. Consequently, a lower number of pregnant drug abusers would lead to an eventual increase in the quality of infant health in the United States. As a result, this would put an end to the social controversy surrounding pregnant drug users.

Then, she presents her interviews as a way of gaining insight into her tentative conclusion:

> After researching the topic of prenatal drug abuse in various scholarly and law journals and reaching a tentative conclusion in support of treatment programs, this writer proceeded to interview two individuals from the Austin community with professional experience with pregnant drug abusers. The purpose of these interviews was to learn more about the topic of prenatal drug abuse and obtain new perspectives on the controversy. Each interviewee was asked eight questions (See Appendix II), which addressed the issues and moral reasoning involved in the controversy. The first interviewee was Pam Johnson. Johnson is employed at the Push-Up Foundation, which serves as a substance abuse center for men and women in east Austin. During her time at the Push-Up Foundation, Johnson has had experience working with pregnant drug users. The second interviewee was Dena Burns, a clinical supervisor for the YWCA of Greater Austin. Burns is primarily involved with AWARE (Austin Women's Addiction Referral and Education program). In her position, Burns counsels pregnant drug abusers, including those that have been incarcerated.

Early in your interview write-up section, be sure to identify your respondents, the organization each represents, and your reasons for choosing them to interview, as in the previous example. The first time you introduce your respondents, use their full names and titles. After that, refer to your interview subjects by their last names only.

As you move on to discuss the specifics of your interviews, be sure not to present your interviews in transcript fashion, such as the following:

> Q: One of the issues in the corporal punishment controversy is whether the punishment is effective. Where do you stand on that issue?

> A: Well, uh, that is an important question. Personally, I believe that it is effective. Research has shown that . . . well let me show you this one study I happen to have here. You can see that, in this study, in 78% of the cases examined using corporal punishment changed the target behavior.

This is not the way you want to include interview material. A transcript-like write-up is more work for your readers to follow and understand because they must determine what is important and interpret the atmosphere of the interview on their own. Further, the goal of this section is for you to provide your own perspective on the interview experience; to do so, you will need to narrate it.

There are multiple ways to integrate your field research into your work, but one of the most interesting is to organize it conceptually. This means to focus paragraphs on ideas and then develop the paragraphs with the material gleaned from your sources.

For example, imagine that Mrs. Elkins and three other interviewees all spoke about the effectiveness of corporal punishment—with different opinions. You might include that information in this way:

> One of the questions that the interviewees were asked concerned the effectiveness of corporal punishment. Interestingly, both administrators thought it was effective and both teachers thought it was not. The administrators seemed to define effectiveness as stopping the behavior immediately. Elkins referred to a study made in the Wisconsin school system in 1994 by the Ladd Organization that showed that in 78% of the cases, the target—or inappropriate—behavior stopped immediately after the administration of corporal punishment. On the other hand, the teachers seemed to define effectiveness as stopping inappropriate behavior on a long-term basis. They pointed to studies, including one made by the child welfare organization Help the Children. These show that, while corporal punishment does usually stop misbehavior in the short term, the same behavior will appear again as soon as the punishment stops.

Analyzing Your Field Research

As part of your fieldwork, you will need to analyze and evaluate the information you have gotten from your respondents. Generally, this analysis follows your description of the interviews. In developing your analysis, you might want to ask questions such as:

- Were the people I interviewed knowledgeable about the controversy?

- Did they have information to support their comments or did they mainly seem to be expressing unsupported opinions?

- What was their demeanor? Were they professional? Passionate? Uninterested?

- Were they open-minded about other perspectives?

- Have they changed my mind about the way I see the controversy and my tentative solution? Why or why not?

This last question leads you to the formulation of your final conclusion. If your field research, together with any additional research, has changed your mind, you will need to revise and reargue your previous conclusion. If, on the other hand, your mind has not been changed and you plan to uphold your previous conclusion, you need to counterargue your position in light of your fieldwork. Counter-argumentation, as explained earlier, means answering the charges against your conclusion.

For example, a portion of this section might read:

> Both interview experiences confirmed this writer's tentative solution to the controversy in support of rehabilitation rather than prosecution for pregnant women. Pam Johnson was confident in

her beliefs about the power of rehabilitation, and she spoke with much enthusiasm and little hesitation. The only shortcoming to her interview was that she gave no consideration to the shortcomings of rehabilitation or the possible benefits of prosecution. Yet, overall she drew from her personal experience and made a strong case for rehabilitation. Like the interview with Johnson, the interview with Dena Burns reaffirmed this writer's tentative solution. Since she referred to her own experiences in AWARE many times, this writer found Burns to be a very knowledgeable, credible source. Also, the fact that she gave consideration to the solution of prosecution as well as rehabilitation aided her in appearing very open-minded to this writer. Yet though her comments on the possible benefits of prosecution were rather persuasive and logical, this writer was not prompted to change positions because she presented no new argumentation or moral reasoning.

After extensive research, interviews, and contemplation, this writer is steadfast in supporting the solution of Side A to offer rehabilitation to pregnant drug users. Both interviews helped this writer gain complete confidence in the decision to favor Side A. After interviewing Burns, it is difficult to refute Side B's assertion that the threat of prosecution can prevent pregnant women from abusing drugs, since Burns cited real-life instances where she saw the success of this approach. However, based on the approval of rehabilitation given by both interviewees, this writer is confident in the ability of rehabilitation to help the pregnant drug users in our country more than the threat of prosecution. In particular, prosecution's risk of deterring women from seeking help ultimately makes a comprehensive policy of rehabilitation the better solution.

Finally, do not feel that you must relegate all the field research to the final pages of your paper. For example, during your final revision of the completed paper, you might wish to refer in the "Presentation of Cases" section of your paper to one or more of the field interviews. Doing this is one way of showing that you have synthesized and integrated all of your research material.

Civic Engagement

The St. Edward's University Mission Statement urges students to analyze and formulate opinions about problems in their world and to take action to help solve these problems.

As a final conclusion to your Capstone project, you are required to take an action supporting the position and policy-based solution you have chosen. This action does not need to be particularly extensive or time consuming, but it should be a meaningful action that connects your project with concrete realities outside the classroom.

In general, the level of engagement your instructor will expect of you for this requirement is along the lines of writing a letter or attending a meeting. However, many students choose an action that requires more involvement because of their personal interest in the controversy. Though you may choose a variety of options, possible supporting actions include:

- Writing a letter to the editor of the <u>Austin American Statesman</u>
- Writing to senators, representatives, city council members, and other government officials
- Attending meetings of involved groups
- Speaking to a group
- Holding meetings here on the SEU campus
- Attending marches
- Circulating petitions
- Giving workshops
- Volunteering

Actions that are *not* permitted as a supporting action (though you are free to carry them out on your own) include:

- *Plans* to take an action (the activity must have taken place before you complete your Capstone project)
- Making a donation
- Signing up for a newsletter
- Anything else that does not consist of a concrete action

Once you have completed your civic engagement activity, you should add an analysis of it to your Capstone paper. If you decided to take a supporting action on your tentative solution and if you had instructor approval, you may have chosen to write about it at the end of Submission Three. However, the analysis of the civic engagement activity usually appears in Submission Four of your Capstone paper, either following your fieldwork write-up and before your final conclusion OR as part of the final conclusion to your paper. Wherever you choose to place the discussion of your supporting action, it should answer the following questions:

- Why did you choose this particular supporting action?
- What did you start out expecting to find? What did you actually find?
- What happened during, or as a result of, the experience?
- How did the experience impact you?
- How did the experience impact others?
- What do you think is the future of this controversy?

In addition to your analysis, documentation of your supporting action must be included in the final Capstone paper and/or research notebook, as appropriate. Consult your instructor for where your documentation should be placed. Documentation varies depending on the supporting action, but it can include a copy of your letter, copies of any responses you received, programs and tickets to events, handouts from meetings attended, or materials developed for workshop.

Conclusion: Revised Solution with Full Support

Submission Four will end with a thorough discussion of your revised solution, accompanied with your own arguments and moral reasoning. This section of your Capstone paper has two very important functions. First, it is where you take a clear stand within the controversy. You should present the solution you have come to support and make clear any remaining details regarding how it should be enacted. You will also need to present *your* reasons for why this is the best solution. What arguments do you find most convincing? What evidence provides the best support? What moral reasoning components (obligations, values, consequences, and normative principles) were most influential to you in making your decision?

Second, this section is also the conclusion to your entire paper. As such, you will need to craft these final paragraphs so they give your paper a sense of closure. There are several ways to do this. Consider using one or more of the following strategies:

- Offer an overview of the entire project and explain what new realizations you came to after conducting your research.

- Restate in some new way the strongest argument for the position you are supporting.

- Relate your conclusion back to your introduction.

- Consider your project in terms of its larger social significance.

- Identify questions for further research.

- Answer the question, "So what?" In other words, explain what your audience should have gained through reading your paper.

- End with a call to action. Explain what your readers should be doing to alleviate the social problem you identified at the beginning of the paper and to ensure the solution you have supported becomes public policy.

The overall idea is to end your paper on a powerful note, encouraging your readers to adopt your perspective on the controversy and perhaps even inciting them to help make your proposed solution a reality.

The following paragraphs are from a Capstone paper on mental health parity (MHP). Specifically, it investigates whether equal insurance benefits for both medical and mental health should be enforced by the federal government. Notice how the writer argues for a specific policy solution and supports his position with his own argumentation and moral reasoning. He additionally discusses his supporting action before concluding his paper.

After completing library research and interviewing two experts on the MHP controversy, I have successfully determined that the side supporting MHP makes the strongest case. Discrimination must be avoided at all costs, even if that means that companies and businesses must cover an increased amount of mental disabilities as well as deal with increased costs. Furthermore, these estimated costs have not been an issue in state parity scenarios, which suggests that cost will not be a problem once full MHP is adopted by the federal government. I am fully supportive of legislation ensuring MHP finally being passed because I have discovered that most of the opponents' arguments, such as cost, discrimination, and categorization of mental illnesses, are refutable.

Supporting my arguments are obligations, values, consequences, and normative principles that are significant in my life. While as a psychology major I have informal obligations to the mentally ill, I also find myself informally obligated to help out those without a voice. In addition to these obligations, I value such virtues as family security and equality. Both are important factors in many of the decisions I make on a daily basis. Also, there are certain consequences that might influence the outcome of my decision. Should full MHP be passed, I would always be assured of equal benefits from my insurance plan, and I would be guaranteed quality and affordable treatment as well. However, if MHP is once again denied, I face the possibility of watching myself or a family member suffer from a mental disorder while struggling to pay for their bills. Finally, I consider the normative principle of distributive justice to be an important guide in making difficult decisions regarding the allocation of social goods. It states that "basic goods should be distributed so that society's least advantaged members benefit as much as possible." Because I believe that denying equal benefits of health insurance violates these standards, I hold that mental health parity should be ensured for all Americans.

As a plan of action to solve this dilemma, I encourage states to continue adapting full MHP so that they can serve as a model for the U.S. Congress. Currently, several states have been doing just that, and the results have been extremely positive. Should this continue to be successful, I recommend that the federal government enact full MHP while creating a financial limit (greater that one percent) that parity cannot exceed. Using this system, discrimination is eliminated, and the opponents are still guaranteed that outrageous costs will not become a problem. Finally, I encourage proponents to educate the general public and promote full MHP because most people are rather uninformed about the discrimination that surrounds MHP.

In conclusion, due to the fact that mental illness could strike anyone, no matter what age, gender, ethnicity, and background, I find it extremely pertinent that the coverage provided by insurance companies and corporations meets the needs of anyone who requires it. Furthermore, I find that through ensuring MHP, a large number of people will be able to benefit both physically and financially. Given that 86% of a large metropolitan city would like to see full MHP passed even if it means that there might be an increase in costs, I believe that legislation regarding full

MHP will soon be passed ("Metropolitan Survey" 1). This would be a significant step for the proponents because it would effectively end the negative social stigma that has surrounded the mentally ill community since the early 1900s.

It is because I feel so strongly about this topic that I chose to give a presentation to Licensed Marriage and Family Therapists of the Austin Academy for Individual and Relationship Therapy, so that they too could become aware of this significant debate and encourage their colleagues to take action on the federal level. Jan Smith, the director of the therapy practice where I am an intern, suggested this option, and I gave my presentation at an April 18 meeting. At first I was extremely nervous about presenting on MHP to a group of therapists. However, the experience was extremely rewarding because after my presentation several people approached me to ask more questions and to tell me they had learned from my presentation. Furthermore, I have joined the National Alliance for the Mentally Ill's website so that I can stay informed and educated on the MHP debate. Initially, I was uninformed and uneducated about the very important topic of mental health parity; however, due to the extensive research I carried out in writing this paper, I now consider myself to be knowledgeable advocate for mental healthcare rights. Perhaps through persistence and dedication to the mental health community, full MHP will one day be achieved, and the negative stigma surrounding the mentally ill will be eliminated.

**WHEN YOU FINISH SUBMISSION FOUR,
YOU WILL HAVE ACCOMPLISHED ALL OF THE PREVIOUS
CAPSTONE COURSE TASKS, AS WELL AS:**

- Locate and interview in person experts on your social controversy.

- Employ effective interview techniques.

- Revise your project according to feedback from your interviewees.

- Indicate how your position on the controversy is warranted by logic or evidence.

- Argue persuasively for your hypothesis.

- Act in a concrete way upon your hypothesis.

Submission Five: The Final Revision

The fifth submission does not usually require any new material. It is simply Submission Four, thoroughly revised for accuracy and running smoothly from page one to the end. However, you may need to add new material to Submission Five if your instructor has noted weaknesses in either your library research, field research, or analysis after reading Submission Four.

You must submit all of the following material with your final Capstone project:

- *Two* copies of your final paper. (At least one of these copies should use your student ID number, rather than your name, on the first page and in all headers and should omit your instructor's name and your section number. This copy may be submitted to the Capstone paper of the year competition or may be reviewed by members of the Capstone faculty.)

CAPSTONE PAPER OF THE YEAR COMPETITION

Each Capstone instructor is invited to submit one or two papers per section to the Capstone Paper of the Year Competition. In this annual event, papers from the spring, summer, and fall of a given year are evaluated by Capstone faculty members. All nominees receive a letter for their portfolio, and the winner receives a cash award and acknowledgment on Honors Night.

- An organized and complete research file.

- An indication on your research file if you would like your material returned the following semester and of the date by which you plan to reclaim it. (No materials may be picked up until after the deadline for grade appeals, and it is your responsibility to pick up your research file.)

Oral Presentation

As part of your Capstone project, you will present at least one oral report on the work you have been doing. Generally the major oral report is given at the end of the semester. Many instructors also require an additional oral report, often at mid-semester. The length of the report usually ranges from ten to fifteen minutes as determined by your instructor. You will likely also be asked to address questions from your classmates and instructor. The presentation is generally given from the podium at the front of the classroom.

The oral presentation is an essential component of the Capstone course. In it you will demonstrate your ability to communicate your research and analysis directly to your audience in oral form. The oral presentation is your chance to display the thoroughness of your research and the depth of your understanding of the controversy you have investigated. It is also your chance to share with your classmates the insights you have gained over the semester and to convey to them the importance of your issue. The ability to express your thoughts clearly and effectively, and to shape your presentation to the knowledge and interests of a particular audience, is a skill that will serve you well on the job market and in your future career.

A final, equally important, part of the oral presentation component is your participation as an active listener in your classmates' presentations. Often instructors will have you complete feedback forms to turn in or give to your peers. At the very least, you will be expected to be present in class during all of the presentations and to actively question your classmates and comment on their presentations when appropriate. This will ensure your classmates receive valuable feedback, and it will help you analyze your peers' projects and improve your own according to your insights.

Content and Evaluation Criteria

Your instructor will give you specific guidelines, but most oral reports include these components:

- An identification of your research question
- An indication of the social problem your research problem addresses and an explanation of why you find the problem worth investigating
- A summary of your findings about each side, including the parties to the controversy, their arguments, their proposed solutions, and their values
- An analysis of each position
- An identification of the side that you are, at least tentatively, willing to support
- A discussion of your reasons for supporting that side
- A discussion of your interviews
- A mention of any unresolved problems or questions on which you are still working
- A discussion of your civic engagement activity—either what you have done or what you plan to do

Evaluation Criteria

Your oral work will be evaluated in two main areas—content and form.

Content (or message) includes areas such as coherence and intelligibility, logical organization, relevance of information, comprehensiveness of information, and plausible and persuasive argumentation.

Form (or behavior) includes areas such as eye contact, volume, rate, diction, facial expression, gestures, posture, movement, word choice and grammar, physical appearance, and pronunciation.

Preparation

One of the keys to a successful oral presentation is sufficient and appropriate preparation. Keep in mind that delivering an oral presentation does not mean *reading* your paper. Yet, some form of notes or outline will help you stay focused and give you confidence. The following are options for you to keep in mind in preparing your presentation:

- Consider using a "key word" outline. This is a one-page outline of your remarks using only important words to move you from point to point. Do not use too many words or you will start reading rather than speaking to your audience.

- Or, consider using index cards with a point on each card. Again, the key is to use just a few words on each card so that you will not be tempted to read your information.

- Many students choose to give PowerPoint presentations. Microsoft PowerPoint is a useful visual aid that can help your audience follow your arguments and provide engaging figures and photographs. However, resist the temptation to use the material projected on the screen as your outline. This will force you to look at the screen rather than your audience. Instead, create an outline for your use at the podium that corresponds with the PowerPoint slideshow.

- If you choose to use PowerPoint, refrain from putting too much information on each slide. Wordy slides are difficult to read and will cause your audience to focus on reading them rather than listening to you. Use your PowerPoint slides as an outline for your reader or as a medium to present photographs, figures, and complicated data your audience may have trouble absorbing aurally. Supplement the outline and other materials with your own elaboration and analysis.

- Remember that practice is crucial. Doing so alone is helpful, but be sure to practice at least once in front of a friend or family member or you run the risk of being disoriented by the audience on the day of your presentation. Such practice will also help ensure that your presentation is the proper length.

- Carefully proofread your visual aid. A carelessly assembled visual aid immediately communicates to your audience a lack of effort and credibility.

Delivery

It is normal to feel stress about giving a formal oral presentation. Almost everyone experiences communication anxiety to some degree. Practice is crucial for gaining a sense of confidence. First of all, it will ensure that you are familiar with and relaxed about what you are going to say. You will be confident that you can deliver your remarks in the time allotted. Practicing, especially in front of a friend, will also help you feel less distracted by your audience on the day of your oral presentation.

In addition to practice, these strategies should help you turn your communication anxiety into energy.

- It sounds obvious, but make a conscious effort to keep breathing. The less air you have, the more panicky you will feel.

- Find a comfortable stance at the podium (or wherever you will be speaking) and keep your feet on the floor. Shuffling and wiggling will not only make a poor impression on your audience, but will also make you feel less grounded and thus more stressed. Walk around while you are speaking only if you feel comfortable doing so.

- Be audience-centered. Your goal is to make sure the audience understands your presentation. If you concentrate on them, you cannot be focused on yourself and the fact that you feel nervous.

- Try to develop positive "self-talk." Consider your "inner monologue" when you think about speaking or as you are preparing to speak. If you discover negative or irrational self-talk, such as "I know that I will just die when I get up there," change it to something more positive, such as "It is perfectly natural to be nervous, but I can use that nervousness to add energy to my presentation rather than letting it defeat me."

- Check with your instructor for other strategies to help you deal with communication anxiety and deliver a good oral presentation.

Online Public Speaking Resources

How to Give an Academic Talk—Paul Edwards, Associate Professor of Information at the University of Michigan

http://www.si.umich.edu/~pne/PDF/howtotalk.pdf

Oral Presentation Skills: A Practical Guide—C. Storz and the English Language teachers at the Institut National de Télécommunications

http://www.csc.ncsu.edu/faculty/xie/publications/oral_presentation_skills.pdf

Oral Presentation Skills—The McGraw Center, Princeton University

       http://web.princeton.edu/sites/mcgraw/oral_presentation_skills.html

Effective Presentations—Jeff Radel, Associate Professor of Occupational Therapy Education, Kansas University Medical Center

       http://www.kumc.edu/SAH/OTEd/jradel/effective.html

How to Conquer Public Speaking Fear—Morton C. Orman, M.D.

       http://www.stresscure.com/jobstress/speak.html

Designing Presentation Visuals—Pacific Lutheran University's Department of Media Services

       http://www.plu.edu/~libr/media/designing_visuals.html

Instructors may use somewhat different criteria in evaluating your oral presentation; however, the sample evaluation sheet on the following pages will give you an idea of what is expected of you in your oral report.

SPEAKER: _____

Style

Volume

Can the speaker be heard? Too loud? Too soft? Is there volume variety?

4 - Excellent   3 - Good   2 - Acceptable   1 - Needs work

Rate

Is the speaker talking too slowly? Too fast? Are there distracting pauses?

4 - Excellent   3 - Good   2 - Acceptable   1 - Needs work

Diction and articulation

Are the speaker's words being pronounced clearly (i.e., no mumbling)?

4 - Excellent   3 - Good   2 - Acceptable   1 - Needs work

Pitch

Does the speaker have enough pitch variety (i.e., is the speech monotone)?

4 - Excellent   3 - Good   2 - Acceptable   1 - Needs work

Facial expression

Is the speaker's face animated or is the expression one of disinterest?

4 - Excellent   3 - Good   2 - Acceptable   1 - Needs work

Eye contact/extemporaneous style

Is the speaker establishing rapport with the audience or is (s)he reading or relying on notes too much?

4 - Excellent   3 - Good   2 - Acceptable   1 - Needs work

Gestures/Body

Is the speaker using appropriate gestures to reinforce the content of the speech? Is the speaker's body position relaxed? Well grounded?

4 - Excellent   3 - Good   2 - Acceptable   1 - Needs work

Audio-visual use

Does the speaker's A/V equipment enhance the presentation? Has it been carefully proofread?

8/7 - Excellent   6/5 - Good   4/3 - Acceptable   2/1 - Needs work

Credibility

Did the speaker seem prepared? To be an authority on the subject? Credible? Interested in the topic?

4 - Excellent   3 - Good   2 - Acceptable   1 - Needs work

Total Points for STYLE (out of 40 possible points): _____

Content

Significance

Has the speaker appropriately indicated why the research question is worth investigating (by highlighting social problems and other evidence)?

4 - Excellent   3 - Good   2 - Acceptable   1 - Needs work

Positions

Has the speaker clearly stated the controversial question that (s)he is researching and described at least two positions in relation to that question?

4 - Excellent   3 - Good   2 - Acceptable   1 - Needs work

Parties

Has the speaker identified parties to the controversy, both general and specific?

4 - Excellent   3 - Good   2 - Acceptable   1 - Needs work

Issues, arguments, and evidence

Has the speaker discussed the issues and arguments of each side? Has (s)he given some of the supporting evidence?

10/9 - Excellent   8/7/6 - Good   5/4/3 - Average   2/1 - Needs work

Plans/actions

Has the speaker identified the sides' solutions to the controversy and discussed their plans for future action?

4 - Excellent   3 - Good   2 - Acceptable   1 - Needs work

Critical thinking

Has the speaker analyzed the strengths and weaknesses of the sides' arguments?

8/7 - Excellent   6/5 - Good   4/3 - Average   2/1 - Needs work

Moral reasoning

Has the speaker analyzed the sides' cases from a moral reasoning perspective?

8/7 - Excellent   6/5 - Good   4/3 - Acceptable   2/1 - Needs work

Field research

Has the speaker clearly presented his/her field research and explained how it contributed to the project as a whole?

6 - Excellent   5/4 - Good   3 - Average   2/1 - Needs work

Speaker's conclusion and solution

Has the speaker discussed his or her own conclusion and solution and provided a clear explanation of how he/she came to this position?

8/7 - Excellent   6/5 - Good   4/3 - Acceptable   2/1 - Needs work

Action plan

Has the speaker taken some sort of action related to the controversy? Did this action seem useful in some way?

4 - Excellent   3 - Good   2 - Acceptable   1 - Needs work

Total points for CONTENT (out of 60 possible points) _____

GRADE FOR ORAL PRESENTATION _____

BY THE TIME YOU HAVE GIVEN YOUR ORAL PRESENTATION, YOU WILL HAVE CARRIED OUT THE FOLLOWING CAPSTONE COURSE ORAL COMMUNICATION TASKS:

- Communicate appropriately in an interpersonal format during scheduled meetings with your instructor.

- Deal effectively with other students in a small group format.

- Give at least one formal oral presentation, adhering to standard communication techniques in both form and content.

Argumentation

The word *argue* tends to carry with it different connotations. Some see arguing as impolite or even aggressive behavior. Others relate argumentation to debate, something used by politicians but not by the average person. In reality, we all argue all of the time. Whenever we express an opinion and give reasons to support our conclusion, we are arguing. Argumentation is a form of rhetoric, which is generally defined as the art and practice of using language effectively, namely to persuade others in a particular direction. All rhetoric, and all sound argumentation for that matter, rests upon four elements: the speaker, the message, the audience, and the medium. With this in mind, anyone can argue just about anything to anybody, with great effect.

Identifying Arguments

The kinds of arguments you will focus upon in your Capstone project are those based on informed opinions. One way to start identifying arguments is to consider what kinds of things can and cannot be argued.

What We Cannot Argue

Facts cannot be argued, assuming the information is verifiable and not a matter of opinion. For example:

- Japan attacked United States military installations at Pearl Harbor on Sunday, December 7, 1941.
- On average, the earth and the sun are separated by 93,000,000 miles.
- Worldwide, 40,000 children die every day from malnutrition.

Impossibilities cannot be argued—that is, situations that are beyond the reasonable demands and expectations of individuals. For example:

- Mars is a suitable planet for immediate human settlement and habitation.
- Juvenile delinquents should have to swim the Atlantic Ocean.
- All Americans must learn to speak Farsi by the end of next year.

Preferences cannot be argued. Preferences at times may look like opinions, yet they do not involve logic and reasoning. For example:

- Vanilla ice cream tastes so much better than chocolate ice cream.
- Greek mythology is culturally more stimulating than Roman mythology.
- *The Munsters* is more humorous than *The Addams Family*.

Beliefs that require proofs beyond human experience or observation cannot be argued. For example:

- God sent AIDS to punish society.
- California will break off and slide into the sea in the near future.
- Alien abductions occur with great frequency in the United States.

for Recognizing and Constructing Arguments

cue words both as a means for recognizing others' arguments and as a way for con-
ur own. Cue words provide the reader with important information regarding the
relationship between one statement and the statement that follows. They are essential to both
identifying and making logical, clearly supported statements. You should familiarize yourself
with some of them.

These cue words suggest that *reasons and evidence* will follow:

since	for
because	as shown by
as indicated by	given that
in view of	for the reason that
may be deduced from	in the first (etc.) place
assuming that	first, second, etc.

These cue words indicate *comparison and contrast:*

despite	in contrast
however	nevertheless
on the contrary	still
though	yet
rather	regardless

These cue words signal that *a similar line of argumentation or supporting evidence* will follow:

the following example	to illustrate
accordingly	again
also	in the same way
likewise	similarly
moreover	specifically

These cue words reveal *causation and conclusion:*

therefore	
hence	so
then	it follows that
as a result	consequently
thereby	in light of
thus	in conclusion

These cue words acknowledge *concession:*

admittedly	granted that
of course	indeed

Analyzing Arguments and Evidence

Components of a Valid Argument

Throughout your research process, you will be identifying arguments in each source you read. As a critical thinker, you should realize that you cannot take arguments at face value. It is your job to analyze conflicting arguments and take a position in the most informed and reasonable manner possible. You may end up on one side of the issue, aligning yourself with the arguments and evidence already established by parties supporting that position, or you may be somewhere in between. The main point is that your position must be supported and balanced by well-reasoned, well-articulated, and well-supported arguments and not by emotional appeals or unsupported claims.

Arguments are generally constructed as a set of statements. The conclusion, or claim, serves as the primary assertion, the statement being argued. The purpose of the claim is to persuade others. It is supported by the reasons, of which there may be any number. These reasons in turn should, under the best of circumstances, be grounded in evidence, such as facts, data, and the authoritative testimony of credible scholars. Finally, the claim being made and the reasons that support it should be logically structured. When an argument successfully presents all these components, it can be considered sound.

Is the Argument Accurate?

An argument may be considered sound if it meets two criteria:

- The supporting reasons are true and accurate, or plausible.
- The structure of the argument is valid.

The following example illustrates the basic components of an argument and suggests the techniques you should use in evaluating its accuracy.

Argument

The Austin Independent School District should allow corporal punishment in schools because it reduces discipline problems.

Conclusion

The Austin Independent School District should allow corporal punishment in schools.

Reason

Corporal punishment reduces discipline problems.

To Evaluate This Argument's Logic

Look at relationship between the conclusion and the reason. If it can be established that corporal punishment does, in fact, reduce discipline problems, does it logically follow that AISD should allow corporal punishment in schools? The following section, "Identifying Fallacies," will provide you more information to help you determine if an argument's structure is valid.

To Evaluate This Argument's Evidence

Look for data corporal punishment proponents have provided to support their reason. Do they show that corporal punishment reduces discipline problems? Such evidence might include testimonials from teachers, parents, and administrators. Evidence could also consist of statistics comparing the student conduct in schools with and without corporal punishment policies or comparing student behavior before and after the implementation of a corporal punishment policy. This chapter's section on "Evaluating Statistics and Other Evidence" offers more information on the criteria to use when examining evidence.

As you sort through and evaluate the arguments you have encountered in your research, remember that there are often no simple or definitive answers. Your analysis will be a matter of evaluating each reason given to support a conclusion and then placing it on a continuum somewhere between "completely true or accurate" and "completely false or inaccurate." Even logically structured conclusions may prove to be untrue once the evidence has been examined. You might ask several questions when considering the accuracy and legitimacy of a supporting reason you have found in your research:

- Does each reason seem true based on your own experiences? Does it seem logical?
- What evidence is given to support each reason?
- Does the evidence provided come from trustworthy sources?

For example, take the statement, "Movies are harmful to children." One problem with this statement is that it is too vague. While some movies may be harmful to children, common sense tells us that not all movies are harmful to children. Another problem is the lack of a definition for the adjective *harmful*. Is the reference to physical harm, psychological harm, or moral harm? The veracity of the conclusion that movies are harmful to children could be increased if the statement were changed to, "Some violent movies are psychologically damaging to some children." *The more specific the claim, the easier it will be to defend.* Finally, in evaluating the statement, it would be important to see what sort of evidence was offered to support the claim. Is it from a credible source? Is it recent? Does it actually support the claim? The following material will give more details regarding how to evaluate the logic and the supporting evidence of the arguments you encounter.

Identifying Fallacies

One way to test an argument is to look at the relationship of the two parts of an argument: the conclusion and the reasons that support it. When the reasons support the conclusion so that the conclusion follows logically from the reasons, the argument is valid. If the reasons do not necessarily mean that the conclusion will logically have to follow, the argument is invalid. It is important to note that the truth or accuracy of the reasons does not necessarily affect the overall validity of the argument. What is being considered is the logic of the relationship between the two parts of the argument.

Consider the following statements: "Former President Clinton is in favor of allowing federal funds to be used in support of embryonic stem cell research. He is a known liberal, and his morals are questionable. It follows then that federal money should not be used to support embryonic stem cell research." This is an invalid argument and a fallacy. Even if the two reasons provided are true (that Clinton is a known liberal and that his morals are questionable), the conclusion that federal money should not be used to support embryonic stem cell research does not logically follow. The reasons may have some peripheral validity but are essentially irrelevant to the controversy regarding funding.

Common Logical Fallacies

In the course of your research, you should be aware of fallacious arguments that individuals and groups may use as a means of persuasion. Politics and advertising often provide the best examples of fallacious reasoning. *A fallacy is a mistake in reasoning—in other words, faulty logic.* Fallacious claims often look and sound legitimate; their force lies in their subtle yet duplicitous manner of manipulation, preying on one's emotions or ignorance rather than appealing to one's intelligence and common sense.

Do not be intimidated by the study of logical fallacies. You do not need to memorize the name of each one, but you should become adept at spotting faulty reasoning as you analyze the arguments of your parties. Further, you should strive to avoid fallacies in your own argumentation. The following is a sample of a few of the logical fallacies philosophers and rhetoricians have identified. Yet, philosophers themselves debate how to classify and define fallacies. Additionally, some statements may fall into multiple categories of fallacious argumentation, thus further complicating attempts to classify them. Consider the following list a tool to help you practice recognizing flawed logic, rather than a comprehensive list or taxonomy of fallacies.

Fallacies of Relevance

One area to consider when evaluating arguments is the relevance of the argument. You may find that there is little logical relation between the reasons being given and the conclusion being argued.

Ad hominem: In this fallacy, the argument is made by trying to discredit a person's qualities or circumstances, rather than by focusing on the person's position or argument. *Ad hominem* actually comes from the Latin phrase meaning "to the man." The example about Clinton and stem cell research given previously illustrates an *ad hominem* fallacy. Here is another example:

Ricardo says I should quit smoking, but he smoked for fifteen years before quitting, and he's fifteen pounds overweight.

Appeal to authority: It is perfectly acceptable to turn to authorities to prove points. However, if we arrive at conclusions by an improper appeal to authority, we are using fallacious reasoning. Some examples of improper reliance on an authority occur when the authority is not genuinely expert in the relevant field or when there are trust issues involving the authority. Here are two examples of fallacious appeals to authority, the first dealing with expertise and the second with trust:

I am supporting the position that animals should not be used in testing cosmetics because Madonna has spoken out against the practice.

The drug company's own study shows its product is perfectly safe, so I don't see any problem with using it.

Appeal to emotion or desire: Often seemingly powerful and convincing arguments appeal to our emotions, but the fallacy occurs because one's emotional response to a person or a position does not logically guarantee that this person or position is correct (or incorrect). After all, when we are emotional, we often aren't thinking as clearly as we should. Thus, there is often little or no logically necessary relationship between one's emotional response to an argument and that argument's veracity. Common emotional appeals are to fear, which involves threats, and to pity, which tries to evoke sympathy. Other appeals may focus upon pleasure or desire. Here are several examples:

The senator began his speech by saying, "If the trade bill is not passed, I cannot begin to describe what will happen to the economy of this state, not to mention this very town."

Mr. Lacy, a candidate for City Council, campaigned at the PTA last night. He told them about his experiences in Vietnam, where he was wounded twice.

It feels great, so it must be good!

Appeal to common beliefs (also known as ad populum or bandwagon appeals): Common wisdom may appear to be a credible support to an argument. It is easy to assume that something most of society believes to be true must be so. Yet, widespread belief is not credible support for a claim unless that claim is about popularity itself. For example, it would be logical to cite a poll regarding the percentage of Texans in favor of toll roads in order to support the claim that toll roads are unpopular. However, statements such as the following that appeal to common beliefs to support other sorts of claims are fallacious:

Jeffrey Skilling shouldn't receive a tough sentence because we all know that corporations engage in that sort of "number fudging" all the time in order to create a successful image for their companies on Wall Street.

Mom, I've got to have a hot pink miniskirt because all my friends are wearing them!

Appeal to tradition (also known as appeal to common practice): Related to the appeal to common beliefs, such a fallacy occurs when someone supports an argument by suggesting in essence, "this is how we've always done it."

Our government has never officially recognized same-sex marriages; therefore adopting such a practice would be foolish.

Argument from ignorance: These arguments assume that a claim is true because it has not been proven false. For example:

I dare you to produce one piece of conclusive evidence that ESP does not exist. Otherwise, you'll have to admit the truth of my arguments for it.

Fallacies of Presumption

Fallacies of presumption are based on illogical presumptions. In general, these illogical presumptions are *implicit,* or unstated. A good way of disproving such fallacies is by revealing the unstated premise, directly calling it into question, and proving it is illogical.

Slippery slope: In a slippery slope argument, it is assumed without explicit and convincing proof that one undesirable effect will automatically lead to another and another—all the way down "the slippery slope" to a disastrous end. Here is a common example:

Don't smoke marijuana! If you do, you will surely become a heroin addict.

Post hoc ergo propter hoc (also known as false cause): Translated from the Latin, this means "After it, therefore because of it." The reasoning here is that one thing is caused by another just because it precedes it in time.

Ever since rap music became popular the juvenile crime rate has gone up. Getting rap music off the radio would definitely improve things in that area.

Circular reasoning (also known as begging the question): Such arguments are based upon an assumption that the conclusion they are attempting to prove is true. In the following conversation, for instance, the salesperson's assertion that she is credible is supported by evidence (Dale Simmons's testimony) that is only credible if we know the salesperson to be trustworthy in the first place.

Salesperson: This is the best vacuum cleaner on the market!

Customer: It's easy for you to say that. How do I know what you say is true?

Salesperson: Well just ask my coworker, Dale Simmons, over there. He'll tell you the same thing.

Customer: How do I know I can trust *him?*

Salesperson: Oh, I can vouch for him.

False dilemma (also known as either/or or black or white fallacies): Such arguments assume an either/or dichotomy that is not necessarily true. You may be familiar with such statements in assertions like "You're either with me or against me" or "It's my way or the highway." Here are two more examples:

Either we invade Canada now or their socialist mind-set will take over America.

Texas must increase property taxes. It's the only way we can fund much-needed education programs.

False analogy: Analogies are often useful tools in explaining or arguing a point. In examining known similar cases, we can often project what might happen in an unknown or untested case. However, the usefulness of an analogy relies on two cases being similar in ways pertinent to the matter at hand. False analogies rest on the comparison of cases that may resemble each other in some ways, but which differ in the property that is being compared.

Compared to men, women are as fragile as butterflies. That is why they should never be allowed to serve in combat situations.

Children are just like puppies. They will do anything for a "treat." That is why the only way to raise them is to use a reward system.

Hasty generalization: This occurs when a conclusion is drawn from a sample that is neither large nor representative enough to provide justification for the generalization.

Several teenagers have recently been convicted of killing their parents. Therefore I support lowering the age at which people can be sentenced to the death penalty to include all teens.

Straw man: Straw man fallacies overlook some or all of the opponents' most pertinent arguments. They reduce the opposing position to something distorted from or weaker than what it really is. The analogy here is to physical combat in which a person knocks over a straw man substitute for his or her opponent and claims victory, rather than engaging the real opponent.

Evolution is ridiculous! I mean, I'm not ready to say that human beings are really just monkeys. Are you?

School vouchers are really just handouts to fund an elite education for middle- and upper-class Americans.

Fallacies of Ambiguity

These fallacies rely on the manipulation of language. Their conclusions can only be supported with an imprecise use of language. To disprove or avoid fallacies of ambiguity, you should carefully define all relevant terms.

Fallacies of composition: These fallacies are based on the erroneous logic of assuming a whole has certain properties because its constituent parts do. While there may be times when such an agreement between parts and a whole exists, this is not necessarily the case. In attempting to determine if a fallacy of composition exists, it is important to consider if there is a logical justification for such a connection. For example, it is logical to assume that if each component of a table is made of matter (or is green, or is made of wood), then the entire table is made of matter (or is green or wooden). Yet, not all properties convey from parts to the whole. Consider these examples:

> I can tear this sheet of paper with my bare hands; therefore I can tear the entire bundle with my bare hands.

> A car produces less pollution than a bus; thus, cars as a group cause less pollution than busses.

Fallacies of division: The opposite of fallacies of composition, fallacies of division assume that because a whole possesses a particular quality, then its parts will. While this may at times be the case, it is not necessarily always so. Here are some examples of such fallacies:

> America is the wealthiest nation in the world; therefore, each American is rich.

> The microbiology research team is award winning. Bill is on the team, so he must be a great researcher.

Class Activity: Recognizing Fallacies

For the following activity, the class should divide into small groups of three or four. Each group should identify the types of fallacies in their list. Once all groups have done so, each group should share its results with the class as a whole.

Group 1

1. Homosexuals should not be allowed to live and work where they choose. Laws protecting them from discrimination are, in fact, tacit modes of promoting degenerate and sinful practices within society. We have well-known religious leaders pointing this out to us. Their opinions ought to suffice to prove this point.
2. If we allow the government to investigate customers before they purchase a gun, soon they will begin to confiscate all our weapons.
3. All of the adolescents who have committed shootings at school in the last few years have had extensive practice with the game Doom. Clearly, video games like that are a cause of school violence.
4. You should not find the defendant guilty of murder, since it would break his poor mother's heart to see him sent to jail.
5. Representative Smith argues for the creation of a national health care system. I can't believe she's trying to turn America into a socialist state!

Group 2

1. The theory regarding the United States' reasons for being in Iraq has no merit. It arose from Paul William Roberts, and he's a kook. Not only is he a reporter, but he's also Canadian.
2. Every time that rooster crows, the sun comes up. That rooster must be very powerful and important!
3. All my friends agree that a Jetta is a great car, so I'm going to buy one.
4. If we don't increase income taxes, we will have to reduce the federal education budget.
5. It's bedtime. Give me any sass about it, and you'll get a spanking!

Group 3

1. If we begin considering theories other than the one the investigative board is pursuing, the investigation will run in so many directions that we'll never solve anything.
2. The electoral college is the best way to elect a president. We've been using it for over 200 years!
3. My friend Anne has pointed out that just seeing the images from video games at the mall has traumatized her young daughter. Many kids must experience this. Therefore, I think we should prohibit the sale of shooter games to minors.
4. If assisted suicide weren't a crime, then it wouldn't be prohibited by law.
5. I know you like eggs, beets, salmon, and carrots—so you'll love the beet, salmon, and carrot omelet I made you!

Group 4

1. Aren't you ashamed of yourself for not buying this car, after I've gone to all the work to fill out the credit application?

2. Students in the 1960s promoted the ideas of sex, drugs, and rock-and-roll. This led to the rise in crime rates we experienced during the 1970s.

3. Stop arguing with me about my drinking. Haven't you ever heard that you'll catch more flies with honey than with vinegar?

4. My rowing team made it successfully across the channel yesterday, so I should have no problem making it across today in my one-man boat.

5. Scientists have never disproven intelligent design, so you must acknowledge it as a valid theory.

Evaluating Evidence

What Qualifies as Evidence?

Research studies and surveys

One source of evidence that comes readily to most students' minds is data gained from research studies and surveys, which involve gathering and interpreting data from large groups. This can be an excellent way of backing up an argument, but remember that credible evidence must meet the standards described in the following "Statistics" section. If there is no data to support a claim, it is important to avoid the appeal to ignorance fallacy mentioned in the previous section.

Precedents

After major research studies have been referenced, some students assume they have run out of evidence. Yet, precedents, when properly used, can be another excellent way to back up claims. Consider that it is rare that a current problem wholly lacks antecedents. When you find precedents from the past that relate to your own topic, investigate how earlier citizens responded. Consider if any of these responses are transferable to your controversy. Review what similarities and dissimilarities might qualify this transfer. This will help you avoid the fallacy of false analogy.

For example, let's imagine you are considering the topic "Should drugs be legalized?" It would be logical to review the prohibition of alcohol earlier in this century when considering your solution. An examination of the Prohibition Era and the eventual repeal of Prohibition should lead you to consider similarities in both cases, such as the rise in organized crime when the substances involved were made illegal. On the other hand, you should be able to discover dissimilarities in the two cases as well, such as the fact that drugs are more deadly today than alcohol was in the 1920s, supporting a position against legalization. Your analysis, drawing on history, should help you to formulate a reasonable position and to construct arguments to support it.

Case Studies

Case studies provide extremely in-depth information on a particular individual or group. Rather than involving the large sample pools used in research studies and surveys, case studies examine a particular event or occurrence. Some researchers select their subject for its ability to serve as a paradigm for a larger group. In such instances the details gained in such a study are intended to give insight into the group as a whole. Other case studies are pursued because they are or were particularly significant in the history of a group or in solving a problem. These studies can often reveal important steps in how the status quo came to be or rapid insight into how to solve a problem. Some case studies are selected because they are aberrant or particularly extreme. These can yield insight into rare phenomena or can be used to dramatically illustrate a particular argument. The details you observe in a particular case study can be applied to broader groups; however, it is important to recognize how the case fits into the larger group (Is it typical? Atypical? Special in some way?) to accurately apply the information.

Expert Testimony

Another source of evidence can be expert testimony. Yet here you must also avoid a fallacy, the appeal to false authority. Be careful to consider the credentials that give a person expert knowledge on a subject. If you choose to include a person as an expert, you will need to explain to the reader what exactly makes him or her credible. For example, if you claim "Dianna Brown says the current economic climate is growing increasingly hostile to small businesses," your reader will wonder why we should take Dianna Brown's word on the matter. Yet if you claim, "Dianna Brown, President of the Springfield Better Business Association and owner of the Springfield independent bookstore Books and More argues the current economic climate is growing increasingly hostile to small businesses," Brown's testimony will seem more relevant and will carry significantly more weight.

More on Interpreting Statistics

A tool used by all researchers is empirical generalization—that is, facts gathered about populations through direct observation. It is just a technical term for using a small sample to generalize to a larger population. This usually involves statistical analysis. In your Capstone research, you will be regularly dealing with this kind of evidence. Use the following questions to help you evaluate the statistical evidence you have discovered.

- Is the sample known?

  The more specifically the sample is described, the better the evidence. For instance, a weak sample might read, "Many young Americans," while a strong sample reads, "Seventy-three percent of students in Austin high schools."

- Is the sample sufficient?

  The sample must be large enough to give an accurate picture of the group as a whole. A weak sampling, for example, would read, "Five out of nine doctors sampled felt that health care workers should be tested for AIDS. Therefore, we should institute a policy to that effect here in Texas." A survey of nine doctors is not a sufficient basis for a state policy. To support the claim that an initiative to make condoms available in public high schools has student support, a strong sample, with a larger sample pool and greater specificity, might go like this: "Two percent of all high school students in Texas were randomly sampled about whether or not they wanted condoms in the schools. The results showed that 67% did, with a margin of error of +/− 3%."

- Is the sample representative?

  It is important that the sample is similar to the larger group from which it is drawn. One way to ensure this is by using random selection. A weak sample representation would read: "A poll of Austin women at the First Baptist Annual Convention indicates that women in Austin favor abstinence-only sex education curricula in schools." However, a strong sample representation would read: "A random sampling of 3,200 women from all geographical areas of Austin indicates that abstinence-only sex education is their main concern."

Constructing Your Own Argument

In addition to analyzing and evaluating the arguments of others, you will need to construct and articulate your own arguments. The position you choose will need to be consistent with your analysis of the parties' argumentation and moral reasoning. Once you have chosen a position, you will need to argue for it by giving reasons to support your position. This requires the skill of constructing arguments.

When we are talking, reading, or writing about controversial subjects, we want to do more than simply state our opinions; we want to *justify* them. In other words, we want to tell our audience why we think one way rather than another. For instance, it is not enough to simply claim, "Executing minors is wrong." If we are to persuade others of our view, we need to give our *reasons* for thinking that our position is the best one.

If we are dealing with factual disputes, our job is usually straightforward. If we say, for instance, "It is three miles from here to Town Lake," all we need to do is measure the distance to prove our point. Such empirical, or descriptive, statements can be proven through experience. Not only is this straightforward, but it is also terminal in nature: By proving the point, we can be done with the dispute.

Controversial issues, such as the ones you will encounter in your Capstone project, are very different from empirical statements because there is usually no way to prove one side is right. Instead, we rely on normative statements that tell us how we "ought" to act or how something "should" be done. Such statements must be argued *for*. Argumentative writing and speaking require the same degree of rigor as do argumentative analysis and evaluation.

As previously discussed, it is important to back up claims with logical reasons and credible evidence. Keep this in mind both as you evaluate the arguments of the parties to your controversy and as you make your own arguments within your Capstone paper and oral presentations. The following steps will be useful in Submission Three (as you evaluate the sides' critical thinking and moral reasoning and then state your tentative solution) and Submission Four (as you evaluate the arguments of the experts you have interviewed and then argue the relevance of your civic engagement activity and state and support your revised solution). They will also come into play when you present your Capstone project orally.

Planning a Strategy and Refining Your Argument

- List your arguments and any opposing arguments

  When beginning any argumentative writing or speaking, it is a good idea to get an overview of your own arguments and those of your opponents. Begin by listing the main points that support your perspective; then list opposing arguments. By familiarizing yourself with opposing viewpoints, you can be reasonably sure you have not overlooked any important arguments before you begin. This will also help you avoid the false dilemma fallacy of inaccurately reducing the number of possible solutions to only a limited selection of options.

  For example, let's assume that your research involves deciding how to distribute scarce life-saving medical resources, such as access to kidney dialysis or organ transplants. Suppose you originally favor a first-come-first-served method of distribution whenever the demand is greater than the supply. You list a first argument that a method that relies on chance is the only way to ensure equality. If another distribution system involving wealth, social status, or potential for making valuable social contributions were used, you argue that there would be situations in which people were denied a chance to live for reasons that were irrelevant and thus offensive to their status as moral equals. You also list a second argument that your method has the advantage of removing from doctors the unfair burden of judging the relative worth of different persons' lives.

  Now assume the stance of devil's advocate. Consider the alternative option of using the recipient's ability to pay for the resource as the criterion and construct arguments to support that position. For example, a first argument supporting distributing by ability to pay is that if the recipient does not bear the actual costs, others will have to pay more for their medical care as prices are inflated to cover the hospital costs. As a result, some patients may find themselves unable to afford treatment, causing a situation as unfair as the one you were trying to avoid. Second, if the ability to pay is used as the criterion, more people may actually benefit in the long run since those able to pay will, in all probability, make more significant economic contributions to society than those unable to pay. A more prosperous society will then be better able to increase the availability of once-scare medical resources, providing more people with a chance to live. Thus, considering the long-range consequences, the alternative criterion will actually better serve the interests of the greater number of citizens than your original plan of first-come-first-served.

  Remember, *you do not have to agree with the line of reasoning you invent playing the adversary.* The goal is to achieve a critical distance from your own thinking so that you can better understand it and, possibly, recognize flaws in your own reasoning.

- Determine your overall argument and sketch an outline

   The following outlining steps are useful as you plan the solution section of your Capstone paper. First describe the course of action you think should be followed regarding your issue. Next, state your value judgments; be explicit in stating the values you are trying to uphold in recommending this course of action. Rank and explain your ethical values in the order of most importance to you. Then, list the arguments and evidence you will use to persuade the reader that your course of action is best and that those who do not agree with you should rethink their position. Finally, construct an outline of this section of your paper. This method allows you to recognize and review the major components of your argument before you start writing.

- Support each argument with specific evidence

   Remember that an argument is considered sound if the supporting reasons are true and accurate and the structure is valid. Pay particular attention to supporting each claim you make (such as those regarding which side's arguments are the most convincing, what values a particular side supports, or what solution to the controversy should ultimately be adopted) with evidence.

   Since nearly all of your evidence is based on research and interviews, you will need to document your sources. Of course, documentation gives credit where credit is due and also allows you and your readers to track down a source should any discrepancy arise or to explore an issue further. Yet it establishes credibility for you as well, so consider giving details about your sources in the text of your paper itself, rather than exclusively relying on parenthetical citations. The same guidelines apply when you are presenting your research orally.

- Avoid objections: Generalization exercise

   Another strategy for testing the plausibility of your position is to generalize from one case to all similar cases. It involves your asking what consequences would occur if all those involved in a similar situation were to adopt your proposal.

   For example, imagine that you are examining the controversy "Should there be further restrictions on the Internet?" Your position involves supporting the establishment of further restrictions. One of your arguments is that the Internet has the potential for weakening national security unless the government can restrict what is being sent over it. Your goal is to ensure citizens' safety. The rule implies that the government should intervene whenever there is the potential for a breach of national security. Now imagine that this policy is extended to other similar situations, such as television, radio, and print media. It is possible that the eventual outcome could be just the opposite of your desired goal for citizens' safety. People might become less and less aware of what was occurring in the world as the government "protects" them. The citizens would be less informed about their own government and thus less able to protect themselves against unscrupulous officials.

   Again, the goal is to become a critical thinker in relation to your position. Using the technique of generalization should help you to uncover flaws and weaknesses in your reasoning and to either defend or abandon your original conclusion.

- Avoid common mistakes in reasoning

   In your reading, writing, and speaking you want to be alert to all the logical fallacies as previously described. In particular, do not let your emotions dictate the course of your own argumentation, which may erroneously ensnare both you and your reader into a false understanding and false appreciation of your topic.

Online Argumentation Resources

Argumentation/Persuasion: Logic in Argumentative Writing—Online Writing Lab at Purdue University

  http://owl.english.purdue.edu/handouts/general/gl_argpers.html

Using Statistics—Online Writing Lab at Purdue University

  http://owl.english.purdue.edu/handouts/research/r_stats.html

The Fallacy Files—Gary N. Curtis, Ph.D.

  http://www.fallacyfiles.org/index.html

Fallacy Page—Bruce Thompson, Ph.D., Adjunct Instructor of Philosophy at Southwestern College

  http://www.cuyamaca.net/bruce.thompson/Fallacies/intro_fallacies.asp

Moral Reasoning

The St. Edward's Mission Statement states that "graduates should be prepared . . . through moral reasoning, to analyze problems, prepare solutions, and make responsible decisions." This charge is a vital cornerstone of the St. Edward's curriculum. Thus, as part of the Capstone Course, students must demonstrate their ability to use moral reasoning to analyze and propose a solution to the controversy they have been researching.

In the fall of 2001 St. Edward's instituted a program titled *Moral Reasoning Across the Curriculum,* based on the work of the noted critical thinker Vincent Ruggiero. This curriculum is specifically highlighted in Freshman Studies and American Dilemmas, and it is the basis of the moral reasoning component of Capstone. Further, instructors throughout the university use this methodology as part of their classes.

An Introduction to Moral Reasoning

As you conduct your research and begin to conceptualize your project, you will quickly realize that your topic is highly complex and dynamic. Indeed, you might at first find yourself bewildered by the array of issues and arguments of the various parties to the controversy, some of whom agree on solutions but for quite different reasons, others of whom state the same or similar reasons to support vastly different proposed solutions. It is important to realize that in analyzing complex problems, the various positions often derive from the different values and desired outcomes held by those involved in the debate.

You will grow intellectually and morally if you take the time to comprehend the ways in which human beings who share values may sometimes disagree on many matters, including social policy. You may also be surprised to observe, odd as it may seem, how people who subscribe to very different values sometimes find themselves in agreement on particular issues. They then become the "strange bedfellows" so frequently found in politics.

Once you have identified the different positions of the parties and understand the case that each presents, you will begin to develop keener insight into the debate if you can identify and think critically about the moral reasoning embedded in the various arguments and proposed solutions. Furthermore, you will need to state your own moral reasoning and understand that, where moral judgments are concerned, we often find ourselves in conflict, not only with others, but sometimes with ourselves. For example, we must occasionally decide to sacrifice personal satisfaction for some greater good, as when we decide we should give up the personal prerogative of smoking in public buildings out of concern for others whose health is imperiled by secondary smoke. To decide on and support your own position in the Capstone project, you will have to understand how the opposing parties have resolved such conflicts. Then, you will do the same based on your own position.

Insufficient Criteria for Moral Reasoning

It is often difficult to decide what is right and wrong in a given situation and to identify what is the "best" moral decision. Many people hold misconceptions about what are appropriate criteria for making these kinds of decisions. Each of the following areas is related to moral decision making; however, it is important to realize that they are not *sufficient* for making reasoned, informed decisions.

Law

Legal systems have emerged from ethical decisions that have been made over time. They are codified reasonable rules for the common good that are made by those authorized by society to make them. However, it is important to realize the respective scope of ethics and law. Not all ethical situations are covered by laws, nor are all laws ethical.

Religion

Ethics needs to be approached on a common ground. Since all religions operate on different belief systems, they do not always provide tools necessary for good decision making. Religion does provide the primary moral framework for many people, and religions often share commonalties regarding various moral issues. However, in a pluralistic society such as the United States, there is a diversity of opinion regarding religion, as well as race, gender, and many other factors that lead to various, and sometimes opposing, ethical positions.

Majority View

Any majority is made up of a wide variety of people. They run the gamut from those who have developed a well-reasoned moral position to those who are making decisions based on misinformation or pure emotion. Therefore, the majority is not infallible, and majority opinion is not a solid basis for making a moral decision.

Feelings

One's feelings are totally subjective and often run counter to others' feelings. Moral reasoning needs more objective criteria to be tested against than feelings. One's feelings about what is right and wrong, however, can sometimes offer a good starting point for moral reasoning.

Values: The Foundation of Moral Reasoning

Defining Values

It is difficult to give a simple definition of a concept as complicated as *values*. Values may be thought of as goods, something worth acquiring or striving for. Values are our ideals. They are what we choose or believe to be worthwhile or to have merit. Values, therefore, should be freely and thoughtfully chosen.

Our highest values are implicit in our ideas about how the world *should* be, while our more trivial values lie behind simple preferences. For example, if a person deplores violence and believes that human beings should always seek to resolve their differences through rational and compassionate discussion, then that person clearly values peace and civility. If an individual values financial prosperity, but not enough to harm others to increase it, then that person may be seen to value the inherent dignity of others over wealth.

It is important to remember that not all values are so lofty. Even when you regularly choose to watch a basketball game on television, rather than a symphony broadcast, you are expressing a preference based on the fact that you think sports programming is "better" than classical music programming. However, your preference will probably never affect another human being one way or another, whereas your valuing peace, compassion, and civility will most likely have an impact on the greater human community.

Perhaps the simplest characterization of values is that they are what explain our actions. Humans are purposive creatures, rarely acting for no reason whatsoever or with no end in mind. If we can identify the purpose of the action, we can then ask what the actor hopes to get out of it or why the action seems worthwhile, and this will be a value. It may take several steps, but unless the person is coerced, physically forced, or mentally unbalanced, we should be able to point to a "good" he or she hopes to achieve: a value.

Values and Ethics

You must also understand that the terms *values* and *ethics* are *not* interchangeable. In the narrowest academic sense, *ethics,* also called *moral philosophy,* is the study of right and wrong. At a functional level, ethics involves recommending and defending systematic concepts of right and wrong behavior. Thus, ethics is concerned with providing people with a normative system, or a set of coherent rules, about what ought to be done in a given situation. Ethics requires individuals to study their moral judgments and moral rules to determine whether they are supported by generally accepted reasons.

From the larger field of ethics, two specific areas concern us here. *Normative ethics* is the area that focuses on the practical task of arriving at moral standards that can regulate right and wrong conduct. These standards involve identifying the good habits people should acquire (how we ought to live), the obligations they have to practice them, and the consequences their actions have on others. *Applied ethics* examines particular controversies, such as capital punishment, environmental degradation, abortion, genocide, poverty, or violence. Work in applied ethics attempts to resolve these controversies by using the conceptual tools of normative ethics. The boundaries between applied ethics and normative ethics are frequently unclear because virtually any applied ethical topic involving particular controversial actions (e.g., abortion) is tied to normative principles (e.g., "the right to life" and "the right of personal autonomy") that are the basis for deciding the morality of the act (Fieser).

As they pertain to beliefs of right and wrong, many values do concern ethics. Yet many values do not; they simply define the things we prize or seek in life the most. For instance, you might value your washer and dryer because you enjoy clean clothes. The washer and dryer, then, are of *instrumental value* in that they allow you to achieve something you value even more, namely clean clothes. We could then go on to ask why you value clean clothes, which would lead us to the identification of further values such as good hygiene, appearance, and making a favorable impression on others. In most cases, if we continue to ask why a person values those things, we will arrive at *terminal,* or *intrinsic values* such as the need for maintaining self-esteem and confidence, as well as that of preserving relationships with others. It is important to note that there is no clear divide between instrumental and terminal values. For example, one person might perceive creativity as an instrumental value used to accomplish the terminal values of a sense of accomplishment or an exciting life. However, someone else might perceive creativity as a terminal value in itself. The terminal values we rank highest are our *core values,* which in turn often define personal character.

To Review

Moral reasoning is the ability to work reflectively and critically through a problem using a normative, or prescribed, framework. Moral reasoning focuses on dilemmas in which an individual must choose between competing values.

Ethics is the study of right and wrong. It is particularly concerned with human duty, what people *should* do in various situations. Thus, ethicists seek to provide people with a normative system, or a set of coherent rules about what ought to be done in a given situation. Ethics requires individuals to study moral rules and moral judgments to determine whether they are supported by generally accepted reasons and thus whether they are acceptable or unacceptable.

Values are beliefs about what is good or desirable and what is bad or to be avoided. Every person has a unique, individualized set of values. However, time and experience influence these, and a person's values therefore change throughout his or her lifetime. When an individual or a society formalizes values, these become codified as moral rules or morality. These rules may or may not be ethical.

Instrumental values are means of achieving terminal values. They pertain to modes of conduct, ways of achieving what one wants in the world. Examples include ambition, open-mindedness, honesty, obedience, courage, courteousness, responsibility, and spontaneity.

Terminal values (also known as **intrinsic values**) are considered good in themselves. They are the end goals individuals and societies strive to achieve. Some terminal values have a social focus, such as world peace, equal opportunity for all, and national security. Others have a more personal focus; they include pleasure, happiness, self-respect, salvation, family security, and wisdom.

Core values are the values individuals or societies rank as most important. Thus, core values help to determine personal or national character.

Value-Laden Statements

When people argue, they rarely state their values directly. Frequently they take their values for granted, as if those values were already apparent to others and no clarification were needed regarding what is good, right, or proper. The means for achieving this assumed good becomes the center of debate, while values themselves remain implicit. It is therefore important to learn to recognize the difference between statements that are value-laden and those that are not.

Descriptive statements frequently contain and describe the evidence that substantiates a claim but are not value-laden. Descriptive statements are grounded in fact or, at the very least, in relatively noncontroversial matters.

Normative, or prescriptive, statements are value-laden. They declare or imply, and prescribe, how something *ought to be* because some state of things is better than another.

For example, a claim such as "St. Edward's University maintains a student population of approximately five thousand students" is a descriptive statement. This is either true or not true; enrollment numbers are not a matter of how one looks at the situation. Conversely, a claim such as "Small classes consisting of fifteen to twenty-five students are best because they allow everyone the chance to participate and demonstrate leadership ability" is a value-laden, prescriptive statement. It prescribes an ideal class size based on the assumption that participation is better than nonparticipation and that it is good to show leadership ability in the class. Advocates of larger, more cost-effective and efficiently managed classes might refute the statement by arguing that vocal participation is not essential to learning course material and that not every student sitting in a class necessarily wants, needs, or ought to be a leader. Hence, we have a debate centering on different values relating to an ideal educational experience.

Identifying Values

Think for a moment about the words and phrases people commonly use when they talk about moral and ethical issues. The kinds of values that are controversial and socially significant tend to pertain to those abstract ideals or codes of conduct that we wish more people would observe. And for the most part, they are the kinds of values and codes of conduct we wish to see in ourselves. Consider the following values:

privacy	competition	compassion	family	peace	justice
security	cooperation	adventure	freedom	prosperity	wisdom
comfort	generosity	tolerance	friendship	individuality	efficiency
beauty	honesty	courage	loyalty	spirituality	charity
equality	civility	order	health	self-reliance	education

Typically, values do not appear in the direct statements of debating parties. Quite often they are implied; therefore, you must infer the values advocated by these parties.

You can actually practice making such value inferences every day and learn to become more adept at discriminating between significant, value-laden choices and trivial preferences. For example, if you notice that your neighbors' house has burglar bars over the doors and windows, you might easily infer that the neighbors place a high value on security. If the bars do not enhance the appearance of the house, you might also infer that they further value security over beauty. If you go to the grocery store with your friend and gather all the ingredients you need to make a cake from scratch, while she grabs a box of cake mix that promises to take only thirty minutes to prepare, you may infer that she values efficiency over old-fashioned traditions, careful preparation, and even the joy of cooking.

Questions to Help You Identify Implicit Values

What good do those holding a given position expect to achieve?
What interests do those holding a given position wish to protect or gain?
What harm do those holding a given position wish to prevent?
Why might the present situation or policy be unacceptable?
What is right, or wrong, with the alternative proposals of others?
If you were to argue the opposite perspective in the debate, what concerns would suddenly become apparent?

Imagine you encounter a person claiming that the federal government should ban tobacco advertisements of all kinds because smoking may cause lung cancer. You decide to role-play the part of the opponent, defending the claim that tobacco advertisements of all kinds should be allowed. What are some of the values you would uphold in the argument? Why is it good to protect advertisers' prerogatives? And which is better—to protect consumer health through paternalistic, federal legislation or to protect freedom of choice and free enterprise through limited federal regulation, even if at the expense of the public good? Taking the time to brainstorm the answers to questions like these *before* you begin will make your moral reasoning much more thorough and coherent.

Thinking Critically about Values

Once you have learned to identify the values embedded within the normative statements and claims of the parties to your chosen controversy, your next task involves analyzing those values in terms of their integral relationship to the arguments and proposed solutions of each party. You do not want to approach the values component of your project in a simplistic fashion. Merely identifying and listing values, but stopping short of a substantial discussion of them, would render your work superficial. Therefore, you must think critically about those values.

Perhaps the best way to think critically about values is to analyze a specific, value-laden argument. Notice in the following examples how certain leading questions may help you conduct a more substantial investigation of the issue.

Conclusion: The United States government should prohibit the sale of cigarettes.

Reasons: Years of reliable scientific studies have established that cigarette smoking causes serious health problems for smokers and for individuals exposed to secondhand smoke. These health problems are, in fact, so serious that they are a detriment to our national economy.

Evidence: Approximately $72.7 billion is spent each year in the United States to cover the costs of the adverse effects of smoking. Health care costs are 40% higher for smokers than for nonsmokers, and smoking accounts for approximately 30% of all cancer deaths in the United States (American Cancer Society).

Question: Do the reasons and evidence support the claim? If not, could this be due to some unexamined assumption about a value?

In order to answer this question, you need to identify the values upheld by the argument. Obviously, the individual or entity making the conclusion values personal and public health. The individual or entity also believes that the United States government has a responsibility to protect its citizens and perhaps the health care industry from those who would sell harmful products. Another value, then, involves responsibility for the public good. However, here is where we might raise questions about the relationship between the conclusion (that the government should take responsibility and prohibit the sale of cigarettes) and the reasons and evidence intended to support it (the studies and statistics showing that smoking is harmful and costly). Does the fact that smoking is harmful and costly automatically lead to the conclusion that the federal government must act? Who else is responsible for personal and public health? The individual is responsible, certainly, for he or she makes the conscious choice to smoke or not. Therefore, while you might agree that smoking is harmful, thus consenting to the reasoning and evidence provided, you might disagree with the conclusion that it is the government's place to regulate personal choice.

Thus, we see that persons holding different values may agree on the facts but disagree on the conclusion about what to do in a given situation. Had we not taken the trouble to identify the values implied in the argument, we might have missed our chance to evaluate the argument critically. We might have merely assumed, by unconditionally accepting the implied value of paternalistic government, that the argument was airtight.

Analyzing Value Conflicts

When two cherished values seem impossible to uphold simultaneously, there is a value conflict and dilemma. Suppose the proponent of the stated argument really believes that the individual is responsible for his or her own health and also contends that the government should not be involved in matters of personal health. However, the proponent also realizes that the issue is somewhat more complex, for research has indicated that Joe's smoking can harm not just Joe, who has made the choice for himself to smoke, but harms his wife, Marie; his children, Billy, Walt, and Erica; and maybe even his dog, Cooper. Does Joe's right to choose whether or not to smoke supersede his family's right to clean air and good health?

Clearly, the prohibition of smoking in public settings has already established a precedent for us to argue that Joe's rights are indeed limited. Social groups may, through active politicking, limit the rights of the individual in the interests of the greater community, and they do so every day. One example is the principle that underlies the seat belt law. Some people will argue that it is their prerogative to risk serious injury by not wearing a seat belt. Yet society, through lobbying and democratic processes, has affirmed the argument that the public good is better served by a mandatory compliance to wear seat belts; the treatment of severe injury oftentimes costs more than the individual can afford to pay, thus driving up the cost of insurance and taxes for everyone else. This same reasoning can be applied to the argument about smoking. The individual's right to smoke is valued by one party, as is the right to breathe clean air a legitimate concern of another party.

In resolving a value conflict, a decision must be made about which value should take precedence in the best interest of those involved. In other words, it is necessary to prioritize one value over the other. This decision usually rests on some higher normative principle (a term that is discussed in more detail later in this chapter). In this case, the proponent of banning the sale of cigarettes insists that individual freedoms ought to be sacrificed in the name of public health.

Class Activity: Values Identification

John Doe works for a firm that manufactures electrical space heaters. His job is to carry out routine safety inspections in the firm's production division. One day, test results indicate that a problem might exist. John suspects that during a one-week period, space heaters with defective wiring were shipped to retailers. The defects can cause fires, so he immediately brings the matter to the attention of his superiors. Further study indicates that the wiring problem, if it exists in any units other than those tested, was confined to one hundred units that went out in a single shipment. The company makes slight changes in the manufacturing process that will prevent similar defects in the future.

There are lengthy discussions on what to do about the possibly dangerous heaters already shipped. Almost all have already been sold. No reports of fires have been received, and company officials are divided on whether to issue a recall of these heaters. The head office decides that a recall would generate too much bad publicity, so nothing is done about the previous shipment. John remains convinced that there is a real danger of fire caused by the defective wiring in the units already in the hands of consumers.

What should John do? What are the primary values on which he is operating? What are the primary values on which the company is operating? Construct a table of the values of the two parties as you consider the dilemma.

John's Values

Company's Values

A Brief Overview: Vincent Ruggiero's Moral Decision-Making Model

So far, this chapter on moral reasoning has focused on the identification and analysis of values. Yet, values are not the only factor that influences moral decision making. Consider the following scenario. You have chosen to analyze the debate over building a fence along the United States/Mexico border and have identified two positions in the controversy, that for the fence and that against it. You notice that both sides highlight safety and cultural identity as two of their core values. Though the sides share some important common values, they advocate completely different policies. How do you explain this discrepancy, and how should you determine your own stance on the issue? Clearly, there are some other important factors to consider.

Vincent Ryan Ruggiero, Professor Emeritus of Humanities at State University of New York (SUNY)–Delhi, provides one useful strategy for making such moral decisions in his book, Thinking Critically About Ethical Issues. You will be expected to employ components of Ruggiero's system in the moral reasoning section of your Capstone project. It is important to note that the Ruggiero method alone does not offer a solution to moral dilemmas. Rather, its use lies in helping you, the analyst, achieve a deeper understanding of the moral lay of the land in which the controversy as a whole is found. For if we are to make reasonable, responsible, justifiable decisions, it is essential that we truly understand the problem to which we are proposing a solution. Thus, while Ruggiero's method leads us to identifying the major components involved on both sides of a moral controversy, it does not instruct us on how to adjudicate between them. As such, it is only a beginning—a part of the discovery process. In the end, Ruggiero's method requires us to carefully investigate *all* aspects of a moral dilemma. A responsible moral agent then has to take a stance on his or her own. According to Ruggiero, three criteria, obligations, moral ideas, and consequences, have historically informed ethical analysis (79).

Obligations

Obligations, as defined by Ruggiero, spring from human relationships. About obligations, Ruggiero says, "Every significant human action occurs, directly or indirectly, in a context of relationships with others. And relationships usually imply *obligations;* that is, restrictions on our behavior, demands to do something or to avoid doing it" (80, Ruggiero's emphasis). Some obligations are formal, like contracts and vows. Others are informal, never formally written or spoken, but morally binding nonetheless. Obligations may develop from a range of human interaction, such as citizenship, friendship, family relationships, and employment (80). Often obligations conflict, such as when an employer's obligation to employees conflicts with an obligation to stockholders. In these cases, preference must be given to one obligation over another (97). When analyzing a moral situation, one needs "to consider all possible obligations . . . before attempting to judge" (102).

Values

In Ruggiero's terms, moral ideals are what we have been calling values. He says they "are notions of excellence, goals that bring greater harmony in one's self and between self and others. . . . they are also specific concepts that assist us in achieving respect for persons in our moral judgments" (80). Some examples of values Ruggiero lists as figuring prominently in moral reasoning are prudence, temperance, justice, and fortitude, as well as the religious ideals of faith, hope, and charity (80). Other important values he goes on to note include loving kindness, honesty, gratitude, and beneficence (107–09).

Consequences

The third criterion is the notion of consequences. These are the possible results of a proposed course of action. They may be beneficial or detrimental, physical or emotional, immediate or long-term, intentional or unintentional, and obvious or subtle (81).

Many ethical systems address the three criteria Ruggiero highlights in some form or fashion. Ruggiero's method of using these criteria is useful in that it provides a clear *system* for moral decision making.

Analyzing Moral Issues in a Systematic Way

It is not enough to know Ruggiero's three criteria; the next step is to use them in a systematic way. Here is a possible four-step process:

Step 1. Study the details of the case.

Keep in mind that circumstances alter cases. Sometimes there are not enough details to clearly determine the three criteria. In that case, use creative thinking to speculate about possible answers, depending on different imagined details.

Step 2. Identify the relevant criteria.

Identify the obligations, values, and consequences. Consider which of these is most important in the given case.

Step 3. Review the possible courses of action.

Be sure to consider all the choices of action that are available. Realize that only in rare circumstances does an individual have just one course of action.

Step 4. After reviewing this information, choose the action that is most morally responsible.

The following example reveals how to use this system to deal with a personal moral dilemma, a situation involving values where all the possible solutions seem to have merit.

You and a close friend are both working at the same department store. You know that Terry's parents recently got divorced, breaking up their home and forcing Terry to live on his own. You also know that Terry is both emotionally devastated and struggling hard to make ends meet. In the past couple of weeks, there have been reports of money and goods stolen from the store. A colleague tells you that everything points to Terry as the thief. What should you do?

Step 1. Study the details of the case.

Remember that circumstances do alter cases. Therefore, it is important to identify relevant questions that involve the details of the case and try to answer them. For example, in this situation, some of the things you want to know are:

- Is the colleague a credible source of information? For example, is it possible she has a grudge against Terry?
- What evidence does your colleague have for suspecting Terry and how did she obtain it?
- What exactly has been stolen? Does it involve a large dollar amount?

Step 2. Identify the relevant criteria.

It is important to consider all three criteria—obligations, values, and consequences.

Obligations

You decide you have several competing obligations. As an employee, you have an obligation to your employer. If you have knowledge of something that is negatively affecting the store, you feel an obligation to take action. (Note: In working through this dilemma, it would be important to review the documents you signed when you took the job. Are you formally obligated to report suspicious or dishonest activity to your employer? In looking at your contract, you discover that you are not.) On the other hand, you also have an obligation to your friend. Two aspects that are especially important here are the fact that you and Terry have been close friends for a very long time and the difficult situation in which Terry finds himself right now. Other obligations that could come into play are those to self, to coworkers, and to customers.

Values

Several competing values come into play in this situation. First of all, there is the concept of honesty (i.e., telling the truth to help your employer stop the thefts). Another related value is fairness. Is it fair to allow one employee to take profits that belong to the company and, by extension, to all the employees as their salaries? In conflict with these are the values of friendship—your long relationship with Terry—and compassion, especially now that Terry is having a difficult time emotionally and physically. Other values that you consider are courage (i.e., doing the right thing despite the difficulties) and caution (i.e., taking time to thoroughly evaluate before taking action).

Consequences

You can see that several possible consequences might ensue from this controversy. One conceivable negative consequence is that the thefts might continue if nothing is done. Another is that Terry might get fired. This outcome might or might not be justified. Terry should get fired if he is actually stealing; however, he *might* get fired because he is accused of stealing, even if it is not proven. On the other hand, your taking action might actually vindicate Terry and put an end to the rumors about him. Taking any action—rather than doing nothing—is probably going to affect your relationship with Terry. Doing nothing, however, may have the effect of making you feel badly about yourself. It is also possible that your own job may be in jeopardy if you are perceived as a whistle blower, but you might have the personal satisfaction of knowing that you did a courageous thing.

Step 3. Review the possible courses of action.

At first you thought that you only had two courses of action available—report Terry to your supervisor or say and do nothing. After further consideration, you realize that there are other options. You could talk to Terry about the situation. You could investigate the situation, trying to find out what evidence there is against Terry and whether other coworkers believe him to be innocent.

Step 4. Choose the action that is most morally responsible.

After reviewing the criteria and your possible courses of action, you decide that the most morally responsible thing to do is to research the situation further. You reject the option of doing nothing. However unwillingly, you have been involved in this situation, and honesty and self-respect require you to take some action. You also reject the option of going to your supervisor. You do not have enough solid information and decide that caution is required more than courage. However, you also reject the option of talking to Terry at this time. He is going through a difficult period and adding to his stress by discussing this—assuming he is innocent—seems somewhat unfair. It could even be interpreted as dumping the responsibility for the situation on Terry, using him as a means to your own end of getting out of the dilemma. You determine to gather more information about the situation, realizing that the results of your information gathering will probably lead to another moral dilemma.

Class Activity: Identifying Values, Obligations, and Consequences

Mr. Peters is a 52-year-old, white male who has been living on the streets for 10 years. He was married at one time, had an intact family, and worked at a fairly skilled job. He does not have much formal education, but can have an intelligent conversation. He is ambulatory and alert.

He has a 20-year history of alcohol abuse and has been in and out of treatment programs, both inpatient and outpatient. None has been successful.

He comes into the Emergency Room on July 4 complaining of jaw and mouth pain. A medical workup reveals cancer of the jaw, and he must have surgery to remove most of his tongue. A feeding tube is inserted to give him nutrition prior to surgery. The attending physician recommends nursing home placement following surgery. Mr. Peters becomes angry and leaves the hospital AMA (against medical advice) with his feeding tube in place.

The next day the ER receives a call from Sister Anne who states the patient is outside on the curb in front of the hospital. He is pouring alcohol down his feeding tube. Police bring him back to the ER two times over the next five days and each time he leaves AMA.

Six months later the patient comes to the ER complaining of intense pain and has lost a great deal of weight. He has nutritional deficiencies due to alcohol abuse, homelessness, and lack of money for food. He agrees to admission. The physician's exam reveals metastatic cancer with radical dissection recommended. Again, the patient leaves.

A review of the history and physical shows that the prognosis is less than six months to live. It is not known whether the patient was informed of this. Your job is to determine what the hospital should do in response to this case.

1. Make a list of the problems that exist in this case.
2. Who are the involved parties?
3. Identify the values, obligations, and consequences of each party.
4. What other information do you need to know about this case?
5. What are the legal, medical, personal, financial, and familial implications for both Mr. Peters and the hospital?
6. What is the best course of action?

Normative Principles

As previously mentioned in this handbook, your Capstone project is centered on a normative question. The word *normative* implies how something ought to be. It contrasts to the word *descriptive*, which explains how things are. A normative statement is value-laden and indicates that one thing or choice is better than another. Such statements usually include or imply the words "should" or "ought to."

When one prioritizes one value over another, one is appealing to some generally accepted normative principle. Normative principles are extremely general so that they can be used in many different situations to help people identify their values and decide which values to prioritize over others. For example, "I value life" is a value statement, which leads to the moral rule, "People should not kill." However, neither statement implies why life should be valued. This is the contribution of the normative principle. In this case, the normative principle "One should act with respect for other people" provides a justification and explanation for the value statement.

The normative principle of *respect for persons* is the foundation of contemporary moral reasoning. This principle implies the duty to honor others, their rights, and their responsibilities. It means that we do not treat them as a mere means to our own ends. It is an important concept in many ethical systems today and has been over time and place. It has been interpreted somewhat differently in various cultures, but it has been generally accepted both by many who identify themselves as religious and by the nonreligious as well. From a theological perspective, the concept of respect for persons focuses on the idea that human beings are created in the image of God. From a philosophical perspective, it focuses on the principle of right desire—that is, we should wish the best for others since they are essentially no different than we are.

From this basic idea of respect for persons stems a handful of other foundational principles that have come to define many ethical codes. They are purposefully vague so they can be used in many situations.

The principle of consistency states that moral reasons and actions, if they are valid, are binding to all people at all times and in all places, given the same relevant circumstances.

The principle of impartiality forbids us from treating one person differently from another when there is no good reason to do so.

The principle of rationality states that all legitimate, moral acts must be supported by generally accepted reasons.

The principle of least harm states that, if we must choose between evils, we should choose the option with the potential for least harm.

Though the five normative principles—respect for persons, consistency, impartiality, rationality, and least harm—form the core of most ethical systems, over time philosophers have identified a number of more specific normative principles that underlie the accepted moral reasoning of societies throughout time and place. Such normative principles will be a central focus for your Capstone project as they are behind not only personal decision making, but also the decisions made within groups, including families, professions, and nations, and thus are extremely pertinent to the sort of moral reasoning you will be undertaking. Kantianism, utilitarianism, and social contract theory are three major normative ethical theories. In order to complete the moral reasoning part of your paper, you need to review these three theories and use the following relevant normative principles in your analysis and evaluation.

Kantian Theory

German philosopher Immanuel Kant (1724–1802) believed that moral judgments must be dealt with by reason, not by feeling. At the center of Kant's theory is the idea that there is a "categorical imperative," a fundamental truth that binds all people. He further argued that the basis of moral action is duty. At the center of Kant's theory is the idea that there is a command—a "categorical imperative"—that binds all people because it is affirmed by reason, and every rational person accepts the obligation to follow reason. Acting out of duty provides human actions with moral value. Though Kant believed there is only one categorical imperative, he suggested it can be formulated in different ways. These three main normative principles are:

The categorical imperative—You should act only as if your act were going to become a universal law of nature.

The principle of ends—Never treat human beings as mere means to an end, but always as ends in themselves.

The principle of autonomy—Every rational being is able to regard herself or himself as a maker of universal law, and everyone who is ideally rational will mandate exactly the same universal law.

Utilitarian Theories

English philosopher John Stuart Mill (1806–1873) was the most prominent proponent of utilitarianism, or consequentialism. Utilitarian theories are based on the principle that "utility," or the greatest good or the most happiness, is the standard of moral judgment. The central idea of any utilitarian theory is that the wrong or rightness of any action is determined by the consequences of the action. People can follow the principle of utility for various reasons; however, the higher motivation is internal, which has been termed "generalized benevolence." To utilitarians, people are moral equals. This means that everyone's happiness is equal, and one individual's happiness should not be pursued at another's expense. The following are the bases of most utilitarian principles:

Principle of act (or direct) utilitarianism: An *act* is morally right if it produces the greatest amount of good for the greatest number of people over the long term. The focus of act utilitarianism is upon ensuring that each individual act produces the greatest good.

Principle of rule (or indirect) utilitarianism: A *rule* is morally right if it produces the greatest amount of good for the greatest number of people over the long term. Unlike act utilitarians, rule utilitarians focus on what would happen if a rule were consistently followed. Example: A doctor encounters a dying patient who can be saved by a kidney bought on the black market (in other words, not through the hospital's regulated and accepted channels of organ donation). An act utilitarian might condone such a practice, in that the transfer would save the individual patient's life. A rule utilitarian might refuse it, in that the regular practice of using organs from unregulated channels could compromise the quality of organs available for transplant, encourage the practice of healthy patients selling their body parts for profit, or make the general public wary of the organ donation process.

J. S. Mill's principle of noninterference: Society is justified in coercing the behavior of individuals in order to prevent them from injuring others. It is not justified in coercing them simply because the behavior is harmful to themselves.

Principle of consequences: In assessing consequences, the only thing that matters is the amount of good (happiness) or bad (unhappiness) that results. Right actions are those that cause the greatest amount of good.

Social Contract Theory

Social contract theory, or contractarianism, emphasizes that an individual's moral obligations depend on the contracts, or agreements, individuals make with each other to form societies. Following rules is in individuals' best interests because such formal or informal laws ensure the social order. Rational people will therefore agree to accept these rules on the condition that others follow them as well. Though precedents of social contract theory go back to ancient societies, particularly the virtue ethics of Aristotle, it is most commonly associated with political theories of the seventeenth century, and its influence extends to the modern day. Prominent proponents include English philosophers Thomas Hobbes (1588–1679) and John Locke (1632–1704) and Swiss-French philosopher Jean-Jacques Rousseau (1712–1778). The best-known modern-day contributor to social contract theory is American political philosopher John Rawls (1921–2002). These following principles appear in many social contract theories and are also encountered in many other ethical philosophies.

Principle of justice: Each person possesses inviolability founded on justice that even the welfare of society as a whole cannot override. These rights, secured by justice, are not subject to political bargaining or to the interests of society in general.

Principle of compensatory justice: Whenever an injury is done, compensation is owed to the injured party.

Aristotle's principle of justice: Equals should be treated equally and unequals unequally in proportion to their differences.

Principle of equality: Each person is entitled to treatment as an equal, to be shown the respect and concern of which any moral being is worthy.

Principle of liberty: Each person should enjoy the maximum liberty compatible with the same for all others.

Principle of human well-being: Each person is entitled to an opportunity to attain a standard of living consistent with human dignity.

Principle of paternalism: A legitimate goal of public authority is minimizing needless human suffering.

Universalist principle: Only if you would agree to allow everyone to do what you are doing is your action allowable or right.

Conventionalist principle: An act is right if it is in compliance and conformity with the rules/conventions of one's society.

The **principles of distributive justice (PDJ)** are a subset of social contract principles that deal with the allocation of resources. Some of these PDJ will be consistent with the normative principles listed previously, while others will be inconsistent. These similarities and differences may help clarify the various claims parties make in a moral or ethical controversy.

John Rawl's principle of distributive justice: Basic goods should be distributed so that society's least advantaged members benefit as much as possible.

Milton Friedman's principle of compensation: Goods should be distributed to each according to what he/she and the instruments he/she owns produces.

Marxist principle of distributive justice: From each according to his/her ability, to each according to his/her needs.

To each the same thing.

To each according to his/her needs.

To each according to his/her ability or achievements.

To each according to his/her effort and sacrifice.

To each according to his/her actual productive contribution.

To each according to the requirements of the common good.

To each according to free market exchanges.

Medical Ethics

The Kantian, utilitarian, and contractarian theories deal mostly with the concepts of equality, justice, and freedom, and thus they have been central to many political ideologies. The following are a sampling of normative principles not mentioned previously that are commonly referenced by bioethicists that may be of use in Capstone projects focusing on the medical field. Keep in mind that many of the previously mentioned normative principles are equally relevant to such projects.

Principle of nonmaleficence: Each person should strive to do no harm to others.

Principle of beneficence: Each person should strive to help others.

Principle of autonomy: Each rational agent has the right to make informed decisions in regards to his or her own well-being.

Class Activity: Understanding Normative Principles

Your instructor may choose to have you complete the following exercise on your own or in a group.

You are chief financial aid officer of a small liberal arts college. Your job is to design a plan of allocating scholarship money. You must choose only one of the following normative principles (specifically, they are principles of distributive justice) to serve as the foundation of the policy:

- To each the same thing
- To each according to his/her needs
- To each according to his/her talents/abilities and achievements
- To each according to his/her sacrifice
- To each according to the requirements of the common good, i.e., to the needs of the university as a whole

Which normative principle would you pick and why? How does your choice relate to your values?

Moral Reasoning Requirements for the Capstone Project

Once you are familiar with the moral reasoning concepts addressed in this chapter, it is time to apply them to your Capstone project. For each side or position you have identified in Submission Three, you will need to discuss:

- The obligations inherent in the position
- The values underlying the position
- The potential consequences of the position
- The position in terms of the normative principles and theories that support it

---

NOTE

Moral reasoning analysis should help you in choosing the position you decide to support. You will discuss this decision briefly at the end of Submission Three and in detail at the end of Submission Four. Each of these sections will remain in your paper in revised form and thus will be part of Submission Five, the final paper.

In Submission Four when you argue for a particular solution, you will need to discuss:

- The obligations that are important to you in taking your position
- Your value system that underlies your position
- The potential consequences of your position
- Your position in terms of the normative principles and theories that support it

As you begin your moral reasoning analysis, note that:

- Moral reasoning will form an important part of your oral presentation, as you discuss your analysis of the controversy and your reasons for supporting a particular side.
- It is not enough to *identify* each component (i.e., values, obligations, consequences, normative principles, and normative theories). The Capstone Course requires that you both identify and *analyze* these components as they relate to the varying positions as well as to your own.
- This kind of work requires you to *think* and to *apply your knowledge of moral reasoning* to your research project. Your research will not provide the answers here. They need to come from your own cognitive work.

Online Moral Reasoning Resources

Ethical Analysis—SEU New College Theory Web Site by Danney Ursery
   http://www.stedwards.edu/ursery/phil2329/2329cr.html

Ethics Updates—Lawrence Hinman, Ph.D., professor of philosophy at San Diego State University
   http://ethics.acusd.edu/index.asp

Fallacy Files—Gary N. Curtis, Ph.D.
   http://www.fallacyfiles.org/

Academic Honesty

Recognizing Plagiarism

The word *plagiarism* comes from the Latin *plagiarius*, which means "kidnapping." It is the unacknowledged use of someone else's work, creating the impression that the work is actually one's own. You are aware, of course, that deliberately copying all or even a part of someone else's work and passing it off as your Capstone project is intentional plagiarism or cheating. Such cheating will lead to a grade of F for the course or other serious penalty, as outlined in the St. Edward's University Student Handbook.

A person can also commit unintentional plagiarism by carelessly handling research materials. For example, suppose a researcher creates poorly organized notes that do not clearly indicate what is a direct quotation, what is a summary or paraphrase, and what is a personal observation. In beginning the rough draft, the researcher may then copy from the notes words or ideas that actually belong to another but are not cited as such. The result is an unacknowledged borrowing of another's work, creating the impression that it is the writer's own. This too is plagiarism and can result in failure of the Capstone course.

Collusion occurs when a student receives, or attempts to receive, unauthorized assistance on any type of academic work. It may be intentional, as when one student writes a section of paper for another student, or at times unintentional, as when a student seeks help from a tutor, who rewrites a section of the student's paper rather than helping him revise it. In either case it is a form of academic dishonesty. People who help you on your Capstone project, whether tutors, friends, or relatives, may help you by discussing the overall problems with which you are struggling, assisting you in finding sources relevant to your project, pointing out patterns of errors, suggesting ways to fix such errors, and reviewing your corrections. However, they should never conduct research for you, write *any* portion of your paper for you, or correct errors for you. Keep in mind that *you*, no one else, should be researching and writing your Capstone paper and completing your Capstone project.

Unintentional plagiarism is certainly more common than collusion and intentional plagiarism. However, all these forms of academic dishonesty will result in serious penalties and must be carefully avoided. To avoid unintentional violations of academic standards regarding the use of sources, you should keep some general guidelines in mind.

- The SEU Student Handbook states our institutional policy on academic integrity:

   St. Edward's University expects academic honesty from all members of the community, and it is our policy that academic integrity be fostered to the highest degree possible. Consequently, all work submitted for grading in a course must be created as a result of your own thought and effort. Representing work as your own when it is not a result of such thought and effort is a violation of our code of academic integrity. . . . The maximum penalty for a first offense is failure in the course, and if that penalty is imposed, the student does not have the option of withdrawing from the course.

   More on this policy can be found online at
   http://www.stedwards.edu/stubook/academic/acad_rules/grievance.html

- In taking research notes, be careful to identify others' words and ideas, whether they are direct quotations or paraphrases. Clearly mark them off from your own comments and questions.

- Within your paper, make proper use of quotation marks and block quoting whenever you employ the exact wording found in a source. See the "MLA Format" section of this handbook or the <u>MLA Handbook</u> for more information on quotation format.
- Following the <u>MLA Handbook</u> guidelines, provide citations in your text and in your Works Cited for all borrowed materials, whether direct quotations or paraphrases, that are not common knowledge. Common knowledge refers to commonly known facts and figures with which you can assume any well-informed reader is already familiar.
- Make sure you understand the concepts of blatant plagiarism, paraphrasing, and transcribing discussed in the following section *before* you begin the note-taking process.

Plagiarism, Transcription, and Paraphrasing

The following examples of plagiarism, transcription, and paraphrasing should help you distinguish between acceptable and unacceptable uses of research materials. We begin with a source for a hypothetical Capstone paper on the abortion controversy.

Original source

In the heat of the controversy over abortion, as assault and even murder become more commonplace, the primary issue seems to have been overlooked, even forgotten—the personhood of the fetus. Is not the pivotal question whether or not the fetus is a person? Some heatedly answer, "Yes!" while others shout, "No!" The answer is difficult, but perhaps it is even more complicated if one focuses on the rational and not the emotional aspects of the controversy. For example, "person" can be defined in a legal sense or in a moral sense. The question of timing, i.e., when personhood is conferred on the fetus, must also be factored in. (From A. B. Rogers, "Blood in the Streets: A Look at Roe v. Wade." <u>Social Services Anthology</u>. Ed. Ryan Metcalf. New York: Random, 1996. 61.)

Plagiarism

Abortion is a heated controversial issue that has led to assaults and even murder. But the main question, the personhood of the fetus, has been overlooked, and even forgotten. Some answer "yes," while others say "no" to the question. The answer is difficult, but perhaps even more complicated if you focus on the rational and not the emotional aspects of the problem. For one thing, "person" can be defined in the legal or in the moral sense. Also the question of timing or when the fetus becomes a person needs to be factored in.

This is clearly an example of blatant plagiarism.

- While the author does not always use exactly the same words, there is a substantial similarity to the original.

- The author does not use quotation marks to give credit when the wording is identical to the original.
- Most seriously, the writer does not give credit to the original author. There is no citation included at the end of the passage, thus giving the impression that what is said and how it is said are entirely the writer's own doing and not that of A. B. Rogers.

Transcription

Transcription involves changing only a few words and then presenting the slightly altered statements as one's own summary of a duly cited source. It is not as overtly deceptive as the previous example, but it is also plagiarism and is not allowed.

> **In the heat of the controversy over abortion, the primary issue seems to have been overlooked— the personhood of the fetus. Is not the pivotal question whether or not the fetus is a person? The answer is difficult, but perhaps it is even more complex if you focus on the rational rather than the emotional parts of the problem. "Person" needs to be defined, and it can be done legally or morally. Also the timing question needs to be addressed (Rogers 61).**

This is an example of transcription and is not allowed.

- Credit is given to Rogers, which is an improvement over the first example.
- However, note that much of the original wording has been retained, but there are neither quotation marks nor the use of the block quotation format—either of which would indicate that the material has been taken verbatim from the original source. The erroneous impression created is that the researcher is *summarizing* rather than directly quoting the identified source.

Paraphrasing

> **Abortion is one of the most controversial issues in America today. Rogers writes that it seems, however, that the emotion of the question has led us to overlook the central issue—which is whether or not the fetus is a person. The question is complex, especially "if one focuses on the rational and not the emotional aspects of the controversy" (Rogers 61). For one thing, "person" is not easily defined. Are we discussing "person" in a legal or a moral sense? Also the question cannot be answered without consideration of the timing involved, i.e., when the fetus actually becomes a person (61).**

This is appropriately paraphrased material, which is acceptable as written.

- Citations of the original source give credit to Rogers.
- Rogers is identified at the beginning so that the reader can recognize that what follows is a summary of that writer's comments.
- Most of the paragraph is written in the Capstone writer's own terms.
- The phrase that is quoted verbatim is properly marked as a direct quotation and followed by a parenthetical citation.

Any material cited in the composition of your paper, be it directly or indirectly, must be included in the Works Cited. If you are not familiar with the proper procedures for documentation, or for compiling a Works Cited section, refer to the "MLA Format" section of this handbook or the <u>MLA Handbook</u>.

Here are a few basic documentation rules you should follow:

- Document all source material that is not your own, even if you are paraphrasing.
- Lead into quotes with signal phrases and proper attribution and with an individual's credentials. Generally it is best to avoid sources with ambiguous authorship; credibility is all but lost in the absence of an identifiable author with credentials.
- Paraphrase as much as possible. Do not overquote. Use direct quotes sparingly and as a way to substantiate your own material.
- Make proper use of quotation marks and block quoting (for more than four typed lines) whenever you employ the exact wording of a source.
- Keep in mind the public domain information rule regarding what constitutes "common knowledge." This simply refers to commonly known facts and figures with which you can assume any well-informed reader is already familiar. If you have doubts about what other individuals may or may not know, document the source.
- See the "MLA Format" section of this handbook for details on proper parenthetical citation and Works Cited format or consult the <u>MLA Handbook</u>.

Turnitin.com

All students in all Capstone sections at St. Edward's University are required to submit their final papers to the online service Turnitin.com, where your paper will become part of Turnitin.com's permanent database. Most instructors will require students to submit multiple versions of their paper. Your instructor will provide you with detailed instructions on using Turnitin.com. You may also want to consult the online tips for using Turnitin.com that can be found in the "Student Information" section of the SEU Computer Help Web site.

Using Papers You Have Previously Written for Other Courses

Because Capstone is designed to be the culmination of the St. Edward's University General Education curriculum, it uses skills you have developed in previous courses. Although portions of the Capstone project may require you to perform tasks similar to those you have carried out in other classes, *the work you produce for Capstone should be new.* YOU MAY NOT INVESTIGATE THE SAME TOPIC AS YOU DID IN YOUR AMERICAN DILEMMAS PAPER. If you plan to use *any* work for Capstone that you have previously submitted for any other course, you must inform your instructor *in advance* of doing so. "Borrowing" from a paper you have previously written for other purposes without notifying your instructor is a form of plagiarism, and it is the instructor's prerogative how much previous work may be used.

TO REVIEW

You CANNOT use the same topic for your Capstone paper as you did for American Dilemmas. If you plan to reuse research or content from anything else you have previously written, YOU MUST NOTIFY YOUR INSTRUCTOR IN ADVANCE.

Using the Writing Center and Other Tutors

The Capstone faculty strongly recommends that you use the St. Edward's Writing Center or the Academic Enrichment and Tutoring Center due to their staff's familiarity with the Capstone project and institutional policies regarding collusion (an unacceptable level of collaboration on an assignment). More information on these services is available in the "Composing a Research Paper" section of this handbook. Nevertheless, some students choose to receive feedback on their project from other sources, including parents, friends, and outside tutors. If you opt to receive outside help on your Capstone project, make sure both you and the person giving you feedback recognize and adhere to the following policies:

- You are *required* to inform your instructor if you are using any sort of non-SEU tutor for the Capstone Course and to provide contact information. Any use of such a tutor without notifying your instructor can be considered collusion. Further, be prepared to discuss your tutoring sessions with your instructor.

- Turning in *any* work that has been written by someone else will result in failure of the Capstone Course. This includes previously written Capstone papers (entire papers or even portions of them), as well as any new material written by any person other than you.

- Tutoring sessions should involve another person helping you to find and correct problems with your work. In this sense they are collaborative. They should not involve simple editing, in which someone finds and fixes problems without explaining them or asking for your input during the revision process. This qualifies as collusion.

- You must be present during any tutoring session. Any session in which you "drop off" a paper to be fixed by another person is not collaborative learning; it is collusion.

Library Research

The Capstone project depends on in-depth research. It will require you to identify and successfully use approximately twenty-five sources. These sources must be authoritative and appropriate in currency and scope to your particular project. Therefore, even if you have written major research papers in previous classes, you should carefully read the following material to further refine your research skills.

Choosing Your Topic

- The Reference Collection on the first floor of the library contains several series of books at the call number H31. Most of these books contain pro and con articles that can help you choose and focus your topic. In general, however, these series are not acceptable sources for use in your Capstone project, although they are helpful sources of topic ideas.
- *CQ Researcher* has a feature called Issue Tracker, a list of possible areas that might work for Capstone topics. *CQ Researcher* is a database available from the library Web site under **Databases.**
- *LexisNexis* maintains a list, *Hot Bills and Hot Topics.* It is a publicly available Web site at: http://www.lexis-nexis.com/academic/hottopics/.
- *Congressional Digest* covers legislation under consideration and the debates surrounding them. Click on **Periodicals/Journals** from the library Web site and search for **congressional digest.**

Researching Your Topic

General and background information:

- *Subject encyclopedias:* These can provide an overview, background information, key terms, and a bibliography of books and articles that have been written about the topic. Subject encyclopedias can be found in the Reference Collection on the first floor of the library and are listed in the Catalog. You can search the library database *Reference Universe* to find entries within encyclopedias in the library on your topic. Some encyclopedias are also available full-text online in *Gale Virtual Reference Library,* a library database.
- *CQ Researcher:* These reports contain background information, an overview, a chronology, discussion of issues, statistics, and a bibliography about various topics. *CQ Researcher* can be accessed through the library Web site under **Databases.**

In-depth information and support for arguments:

- *Books:* Books can contain overviews of the topic, background information about the controversy, evidential data, parties to the issue, and more. Books can be found by using these tools available from the library Web site:
  - **Library Catalog** (books owned by the library)
  - **NetLibrary** (e-books)
  - **WorldCat** (books owned by libraries around the world, available through Interlibrary Loan)

- *Articles:* Articles can contain research studies, evidential data, as well as commentary. They can be found by searching the online databases accessible from the library Web site under **Databases.** Strategies for searching the databases are found in "**Online Search Strategies,**" later in this section.
  - *Academic Search Premier* and *Expanded Academic ASAP:* These two databases cover a wide range of topics and include both popular and scholarly articles (see the following section on "**Scholarly vs. Popular**" for more information).
  - *Subject Databases:* Also available are numerous subject databases that provide specialized coverage of an area such as Business, Education, Health & Medicine, and Legal. Subject listings of the databases are accessed from the bottom of the **Databases** page under "**By Subject, Discipline or Format.**"

  Finding full text: When the full text of the article is available in the database, there will be a link to the HTML or PDF text. When the full text isn't available, there will often be a link to "**Check for Full Text.**" Clicking this link will search the library's collection. There are two kinds of results. One result, "**0 records found,**" means the journal is not in the library. See the section "**If the Library Does Not Have a Book or Article**" for information on how to obtain the article. The other kind of result is a record indicating the availability of full text in a database, paper, or microform. Check the date ranges listed in the result to see if your article can be obtained. If the article falls outside the date ranges, see the section "**If the Library Does Not Have a Book or Article.**"

  - *Statistical Resources:* Statistical data can be found in many sources, including within articles. Major sources include *Information Plus* books (Reference Collection; *Gale Virtual Reference Library*); *FedStats* (http://www.fedstats.gov); and the *Statistical Abstract of the United States* (Reference Collection and http://www.census.gov/compendia/statab/). For additional sources of statistical data, consult the research guide "**Finding Statistics**" on the library Web site under **Research Guides.**

Public policy:

Policy can be laws, court decisions, and even proposals designed by knowledgeable people to solve social problems and then published in a public forum.

- Legislation
  - *Bills and Laws:* To find proposed and current federal legislation, you can use *LexisNexis Congressional* (a library database) or the *THOMAS* Web site (http://thomas.loc.gov). To find state legislation, you can search state legislature Web sites.
  - *Legal Opinion:* To find informed opinion by legal experts, you can search *LegalTrac, Legal Collection,* and the "Legal Research" section of *LexisNexis Academic.* These are library databases available from the library Web site under **Databases.**
  - *Legislative Analysis:* To find overviews and analysis of legislation, you can search for Congressional Research Service documents at http://www.opencrs.com, or search *CQ Public Affairs Collection,* a library database available from the library Web site under **Databases.**
  - *Congressional Debate:* To find congressional debate on legislation, you can access the Congressional Record in *LexisNexis Congressional,* a library database available from the library Web site under **Databases.**
- Court Cases
  - *Identifying Court Cases:* Major sources to find court cases include: *CQ Supreme Court Collection* (a library database), *West's Encyclopedia of American Law* (in *Gale Virtual Reference Library,* a library database), or books about court cases in the Reference Collection (search

the library catalog for cases and limit the location to Reference). Cases may also be mentioned in law review articles or other scholarly articles.

- *Court Opinion:* To read judges' rulings on court cases, search Case Law within the "Legal Research" section of *LexisNexis Academic.*

- *Case Analysis:* To find expert opinion and analysis of court cases, you can search *CQ Supreme Court Collection, LegalTrac,* and *Legal Collection,* library databases available from the library Web site under **Databases.**

- *Congressional Testimony:* To find the transcript of expert witness testimony to congressional hearings and committees, you can search the "Hearings" section in the Advanced Search of *LexisNexis Congressional,* or add the word **testimony** to a keyword search in Google Government (http://www.google.com/ig/usgov).

- *Public Policy Research Reports:* Reports on public policy, including analysis and solutions to public policy issues, are often written by think tanks and research organizations. These reports may reflect the organization's bias, so be sure to investigate the organization's mission and consider this bias when you are working on the analysis section of your Capstone project. To find these reports, you can search *PolicyFile* (a library database) and Google. To search Google for these reports, limit your search to ".org" domains by following your keyword(s) with **site:.org.** For example:

illegal immigrants site:.org

The Congressional Research Service (CRS) also writes reports on public policy. These reports include nonbiased analysis on legislation, as well as issue definitions and background. You can find CRS reports using *OpenCRS* (http://www.opencrs.com).

Parties to the controversy and issues, arguments, and evidence

- *CQ Researcher:* You can find references to parties and issues embedded within the text of *CQ Researcher* reports. *CQ Researcher* is a database available from the library Web site under **Databases.**

- *LexisNexis Congressional:* Contains testimony to Congressional hearings and committees by expert witnesses and parties to the controversy as well as transcripts of Congressional debates. *LexisNexis Congressional* is a library database available from the library Web site under **Databases.**

- *Advocacy Web sites:* Many advocacy groups have Web sites that express their positions on controversial issues of importance to them. These can be found by conducting a Google search. You can limit your Google search to ".org" domains by following your keyword(s) with **site:.org.** For example:

illegal immigrants site:.org

Online Search Strategies

Keyword Searching

The Catalog and every online database in the library allow the use of keyword searching. A keyword search tells the database to find every record containing the search terms entered. Note that the full text of the book or article is not searched, only fields such as the title, author, abstract (summary), and subject terms.

A single search term, such as **marriage,** or a phrase such as **gay marriage** can be used. The use of quotation marks to denote a phrase is not supported in all databases, but often the database recognizes two words next to each other as a phrase.

Keyword search Academic Search Premier	Results for: gay marriage Find: gay marriage　　　in [Select a Field (optional) ▼] [Search] 1-10 of 2003 Page: 1 2 3 4 5 Next

Keyword searches tend to be broad and often generate many results. Some results will be applicable to the topic and some might be unrelated. Here are strategies to improve your search results.

Focusing the Search

- **Boolean logic** allows one to refine keyword searches for more targeted results. The most common Boolean operators are *or* and *and.*

  - *or* is used to broaden a search (yield more results) by including similar terms. Example:

    gay marriage **or** same-sex marriage

  - *and* is used to narrow a search (yield fewer results) by introducing another concept. Example:

    gay marriage **and** legislation

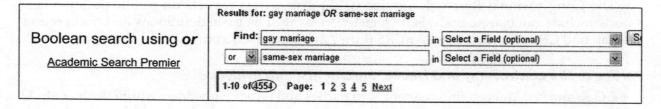

Boolean search using *or* Academic Search Premier	Results for: gay marriage *OR* same-sex marriage Find: gay marriage　　　in [Select a Field (optional) ▼] [S or ▼ same-sex marriage　　in [Select a Field (optional) ▼] 1-10 of 4554 Page: 1 2 3 4 5 Next

- **Field-specific searching:** Each individual record is composed of a group of fields. The title field contains only the item's title, the subject field contains subject terms assigned to that item, etc. In a **keyword search** the term may be found anywhere in the record, but in a **specific field search** the term must be found in the specified field, such as subject, title, or abstract.

- **Subject headings** are assigned to books in the Library Catalog and to periodical articles in the library's online databases. They indicate what a book or article is about. The Library Catalog and each database have their own list of specific terms that may be used as subject headings. This is called *controlled vocabulary.* For example:

Common usage	Controlled Subject Heading
gay marriage	same-sex marriage

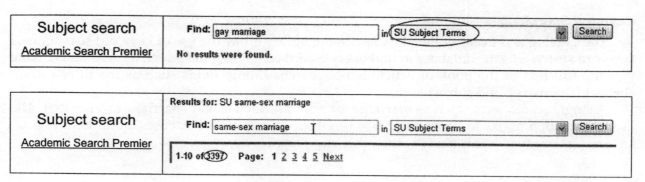

Subject search Academic Search Premier	Find: gay marriage　　　in SU Subject Terms ▼ [Search] No results were found.

Subject search Academic Search Premier	Results for: SU same-sex marriage Find: same-sex marriage　　in SU Subject Terms ▼ [Search] 1-10 of 3397 Page: 1 2 3 4 5 Next

- Subject headings are usually a link. If you click on them, the database will bring up all the items that have been assigned that exact subject heading.
- Take note of the subject headings assigned to any item that is especially useful. These headings may be used as search terms in the subject field to find additional books and articles.

Combination search Academic Search Premier	**Results for:** SU same-sex marriage *AND* SU (law *OR* legislation) *AND* (united states *OR* u.s.) **Find:** `same-sex marriage` in `SU Subject Terms` ▼ `Search` and ▼ `law or legislation` in `SU Subject Terms` ▼ and ▼ `united states or u.s.` in `Select a Field (optional)` ▼ 1-10 of 952 Page: 1 2 3 4 5 Next

Scholarly Versus Popular Sources

Capstone requires you to use authoritative, rather than popular, resources in your project. All Capstone projects are unique and will need to be developed using a variety of types of resource materials. However, many will require the use of what are called "scholarly" sources. Here are some guidelines for distinguishing between popular and scholarly resources. If you're still not sure, your professor or a librarian can help you determine whether an article or book is scholarly.

Popular Magazine Articles

- Are written for the general public to inform or entertain
- Rely on basic vocabulary words
- Are generally written by journalists
- Often contain photographs and other images
- Seldom contain references, footnotes, and bibliographies
- Examples: articles from *Newsweek, People,* and *Money*

Scholarly Journal Articles

- Are written by experts in the field for those who have some prior knowledge of the area being discussed
- Always include a list of references of the sources the author has used and often contain footnotes and endnotes
- Are frequently more than ten pages
- Usually do not include pictures, although may include graphs or charts
- Use technical, specialized vocabulary
- Are chosen, reviewed, and edited by one or more other experts in the field (i.e., they are "peer reviewed")
- Examples: feature articles from *Community Mental Health Journal, Journal of Pastoral Care,* and *Journal of the American Medical Association (JAMA)*

Popular and Scholarly Books

Books can be popular or scholarly as well. In particular, scholarly books contain citations and have footnotes, endnotes, or some other form of documentation. You can use the criteria in the following section, "A Guide for Evaluating Information Sources," to determine whether books are scholarly. If you are still unsure whether a book is scholarly or popular, consult with your professor or a librarian.

Newspapers

Some Capstone topics may require you to use newspapers, especially to find current information on your topic. If you need to reference information in newspapers, choose ones that are considered particularly credible, such as the *New York Times*, the *Washington Post*, the *Wall Street Journal*, the *Los Angeles Times*, and the *Christian Science Monitor*. Capstone topics that are specific to Texas may require you to reference Texas newspapers, and two respected ones are the *Dallas Morning News* and the *Houston Chronicle*. Austin-specific topics will require you to reference the *Austin-American Statesman* and possibly the *Austin Chronicle*.

Web Sites

Web sites can be valuable sources of information, but they have to be carefully evaluated. Credible sites have been recently updated and include clear authorship and responsibility for content. Generally, the web sites of government agencies; accredited academic institutions; and credible organizations, such as the American Medical Association (AMA) or the American Civil Liberties Union (ACLU), are considered acceptable. Wikipedia is not an acceptable site as it does not meet the above standards.

Government Organizations

Many government agencies and organizations can provide vital information on your Capstone topic, such as:

Library of Congress (an excellent source of information about federal topics)

Congressional Research Service

Government Accountability Office (GAO)

National Conference of State Legislators (NCSL)

National Governors Association

A Guide for Evaluating Information Sources

Just because a book, article, or Web site matches your search criteria doesn't mean that it is an appropriate or reliable source of information. Here are some basic criteria for determining the quality of a source.

Authority

- Who is the author and what are his or her credentials? What is his or her educational background or experience?
- With what institutions or organizations is the author affiliated?
- Does the author use adequate documentation (references, bibliography, credits, footnotes, etc.) to support his or her work?

Content

- What evidence or documentation is presented to support the author's arguments?
- Are arguments and supporting evidence presented clearly and logically?
- Is the topic covered comprehensively or partially, or is it a broad overview?
- Is the work free of spelling, grammatical, and typographical errors?

Relevancy

- How current is the text? (Note: currency is more important for some topics than others.)
- What kind of audience is the author addressing? Is it aimed at a general or specialized audience?
- Is the source appropriate for your specific research needs?

Objectivity

- Are the author's arguments based on logic, or are they appeals to the reader's emotions?
- Is the work intended to inform the reader or to sway his or her opinion?
- Are issues treated in a factual manner?

If the Library Does Not Have a Book or Article

Interlibrary Loan and **TexShare** are the services that provide you with books or articles not owned by the Scarborough-Phillips Library.

Interlibrary Loan (ILL) is the service of borrowing books, journal articles, and other materials from other libraries when items are not available in the Scarborough-Phillips Library collection. Requests are placed using ILLiad, a Web-based system accessed from the library Web site. You must create a user account to use ILLiad for the first time. For each request, you must supply a full and accurate bibliographic citation.

- When an article or book chapter is requested, you will receive an e-mail message usually within a week directing you to check your ILLiad account to access the requested material in PDF format.
- When a book is requested, you will receive an e-mail message in about ten days informing you the book is available at the library.
- Sometimes books and articles are very difficult to find or impossible to borrow. If the library cannot procure an item for you, you will receive an e-mail notice advising you of this as soon as possible.
- This service is normally free. If there is a charge, you will be consulted before a charge is incurred.

TexShare is a cooperative program to share library resources. The members of TexShare include most academic and public libraries in Texas. These libraries extend free reciprocal borrowing privileges to each other's patrons.

- TexShare cards will be issued to St. Edward's University students whose records indicate a history of responsible use of library materials.
- You may apply for a TexShare Card in person at the Circulation Desk or from the library Web site. *Please allow one (1) business day to process the application.*
- TexShare cards issued to students will expire at the end of each semester on May 15, August 15, or December 15.
- Present your TexShare card to the Circulation Desk of the library at which you wish to borrow materials and you will be issued a courtesy borrowers card. In addition, you will be asked to present a valid SEU ID card or other identification. Ordinarily, patrons with TexShare cards will not be allowed to check out material between semesters at other academic libraries.
- **A courtesy card does not allow remote access to electronic resources.**

Research Assistance

Research assistance is available at the Reference Desk, by phone (448-8474), or by e-mail (refdesk@stedwards.edu). Reference hours are posted on the library Web site under **Research Assistance.**

Reference appointments: If after working with a librarian at the Reference Desk, you need more in-depth assistance, contact Reference Services via online, phone, or in person to discuss scheduling an appointment.

Online Research Resources

Resources for Evaluating Web Sites

Evaluating Web Sites: Criteria and Tools—Cornell University Library
  http://www.library.cornell.edu/olinuris/ref/research/webeval.html

Evaluating Web Pages: Techniques to Apply & Questions to Ask—UC Berkeley Library
  http://www.lib.berkeley.edu/TeachingLib/Guides/Internet/Evaluate.html

Evaluating Information Found on the Internet—Elizabeth E. Kirk, Johns Hopkins University Library
  http://www.library.jhu.edu/researchhelp/general/evaluating/index.html

Thinking Critically about Web Page Content—Michigan State University Libraries
  http://www.lib.msu.edu/link/critical.htm

Activities for Evaluating Web Pages

Web Page Evaluation Checklist—Joe Barker, UC Berkeley Library
  http://www.lib.berkeley.edu/TeachingLib/Guides/Internet/EvalForm_General_Barker.pdf

Criteria for Evaluating Web Resources—Kent State University Library Worksheet can be found in PDF, Microsoft Word, or RTF format at:
  http://www.library.kent.edu/page/10475

ICYouSee: T is for Thinking: A Guide to Critical Thinking About What You See on the Web—John R. Henderson, Ithica College Library
  Overall Site: http://www.ithaca.edu/library/training/think.html
  Web Site Comparison Quiz: http://www.ithaca.edu/library/training/think8.html
  Web Site Evaluation Assignment: http://www.ithaca.edu/library/training/think7.html

Resources for Evaluating Scholarly Sources

Critically Analyzing Information Sources—Cornell University Library
  http://www.library.cornell.edu/olinuris/ref/research/skill26.htm

Composing a Research Paper

By the time you reach the Capstone course, you will likely have written a number of research papers. Therefore, the information in this section should be a review of skills you have already developed. This chapter will cover three areas to help you hone those skills:

- Organization
- Style
- Grammar, spelling, and punctuation

Local Resources for Help

There are several resources for help with writing on the St. Edward's campus:

Your instructor: The comments your instructor writes on your paper are a summary of its strengths and weaknesses. He or she will also give you detailed insight into how you can improve in the course in face-to-face scheduled meetings. Your course syllabus will provide information on the best way to set up additional appointments if you need further guidance.

The Writing Center: The St. Edward's University Writing Center is an excellent resource for you during all stages of the writing process. Instructors can help you brainstorm topics, organize your paper, write content, or revise. While normally students are only permitted to sign up for one 30-minute session at a time, Capstone students may sign up for an hourlong session by booking two back-to-back sessions with the same tutor. Students are permitted two sessions per week, and Writing Center services are free to you as a St. Edward's student. All scheduling for the Writing Center takes place online through its Web site at:

http://www.stedwards.edu/writing/index.html

Here are some suggestions for getting the most out of your Writing Center session:

- Try to sign up for Writing Center sessions one to two weeks in advance. The Writing Center tutors may become booked up around the time of Capstone paper deadlines.

- Bring everything that may be useful in writing your paper with you. This should always include your Capstone handbook, any additional assignment information your instructor has distributed, and a hard copy of your paper. You may also want to bring copies of relevant sources and your instructor's comments on your previous draft.

- An hour may sound long, but it is not enough time for a tutor to read and give you feedback on an entire Capstone paper. In fact, at some stages of the paper writing process, the tutors may need to spend the entire hour discussing only a few pages with you. Plan *multiple* visits rather than expecting tutors to "fix" your paper in one sitting.

- If you are more than ten minutes late, your appointment will be given to another student. If you miss more than two appointments, you will be blocked from scheduling appointments for the remainder of the semester.

- You must use the online scheduler to cancel appointments. Log in to it, then select "My Schedule" at the top of the page. It will show you the Writing Center appointments for which you are scheduled and allow you the option to cancel them.

- If you need to get into the Writing Center at the last minute, try a walk-in appointment slot. These times are listed on the online schedule. Walk-in slots will be given to students on a first come, first serve basis.

- Keep in mind there are a variety of tutors at the Writing Center with a variety of different teaching styles. Try visiting several different people to find an approach that works best for you.

Academic Enrichment and Tutoring Center: Academic Planning and Support Services provides tutoring through the Academic Enrichment and Tutoring Center. Students may qualify for free tutors; otherwise, the cost is $7.50 per hour. Call the Tutoring Center at 637-1996 or stop by Moody Hall 122 to get more information.

DON'T WAIT!

If you need help with your writing, get it now. The situation will not get any better if you procrastinate—and the skills you learn will last a lifetime.

Organization

Your Capstone paper requires extensive research. One of the challenges you face even before you start writing is organizing this information. Time spent on organization in the early stages of the project will definitely yield rewards later in the semester.

Note taking and outlining, two organizational strategies for planning your Capstone—or any other—research paper, are discussed in the following sections.

Note Taking

Note taking is pivotal to your success in the Capstone project. Some of you may be operating under the misconception that photocopying the pages of a book or marking an article with a highlighter is the same as note taking. These are merely steps in the note-taking process, but you must do much more than this to take accurate notes reflecting both the content of the original source *and* your analysis of its relationship to your project. Keep in mind that a good researcher strives to be both ethical and efficient. Thorough notes help a writer avoid plagiarism. Also, while detailed notes may take some time and energy at the beginning of a research project, they save even more time later. A successful researcher is one who follows these steps:

- Use the same medium for taking all the notes for a given project. Choose what works for you—index cards, a notebook, a legal pad, etc.—but consider the following information as you make your decision.

  - The use of index cards is a standard research technique. They are easy to organize, and their relatively small size encourages writers to organize and consolidate their thoughts before writing. In addition, they come in a variety of colors that can help identify material relating to various sections of your research project.

  - If you opt to take notes in a notebook, one with removable pages (such as a three-ring binder) is preferable so that pages can be moved around as required. A different page should be used for each new source.

  - If you choose to use a legal pad or spiral notebook, at some point in the research process you will likely want to remove the pages and organize them in an accordion file or other organizational device according to topic.

  - Some students choose to annotate the articles themselves. This is an acceptable method of note taking *if, and only if,* you truly annotate the articles. In other words, you must add any missing bibliographic information to the article and write your own summary (perhaps at the top of the page) and analysis (at the appropriate paragraphs) in addition to highlighting and underlining.

- At the top of each card or page, put the complete bibliographic information for the source you are researching. Some writers like to organize that information into correct MLA form right away, while others prefer to leave that task until later. The key is to document all the bibliographic information so that you do not have to waste time looking for it later. Do not take any shortcuts here!

  - If you are researching from a book, you must include:

  -the author's name (or the editor's name, if applicable)

  -the title of the book

  -the edition (if applicable)

  -the series title and volume number (if applicable)

-the place of publication

-the publisher

-the date of publication

-the pages of the book you used in your research (if you did not use the entire book, but only an article or chapter from an anthology or collection)

- If you are researching from a periodical article, be sure to include:

-the author's name

-the title of the article

-the source or the article (i.e., the name of the journal, magazine, or newspaper)

-the volume and issue number (if scholarly journal)

OR

-the date of publication (if a non-scholarly periodical)

-the pages on which the article appears

- If you secured an article from a subscription service or online database, then you must *add* the following to your bibliographic information:

-the name of the database (if part of a larger service)

-the name of the subscription service

-the name of the library (if applicable)

-the city and state of the library (if applicable)

-the date you accessed the database

[A URL is *not* required for a library subscription service.]

- If you are researching from a Web site, be sure to include:

-the name of the author who created the content of the Web site or Web page (if known) [generally this is *not* the same as the "Webmaster"]

-the title of the Web site or web page

-the title of the Web site of which the page is a part (if applicable)

-the date of publication or last revision (if known)

-the name of the institution or organization associated with the site (if applicable)

-the date you accessed the Web site

-the URL

-all the information relating to the work's initial publication if the work was originally

   published elsewhere

NOTE

See the MLA Handbook or the "MLA Format" section of this guide for additional examples of information needed.

- After noting the bibliographic information, *summarize the source* you have read. The goal here is for you to "digest" the information and put it into your own words. Not only does this ensure that you completely understand the material you are reading, but also this summarized material is easy for you to refer back to and work with later. Additionally, note who the author is—a Harvard economics professor? A United Nations lawyer? A politician? A journalist? Part of recognizing a credible source is knowing whether the author has any expertise in the subject.

- Your notes should *not be too wordy*. You want to synthesize the information you are researching, not merely copy it; therefore, what you write down will be considerably shorter than the original text. On the other hand, your notes should *not be too skimpy*. Notes that are too brief will not give you enough to work with later on; therefore, you should include at least a few sentences of your own analysis in the notes you take for each source.

- Be sure to carefully *note the page numbers* of the material you are researching. This applies both to information you plan to quote and to information you plan to paraphrase. You will need the page numbers for the parenthetical citations used throughout your research paper.

REMEMBER!

You need page numbers whether you are using direct quotation or paraphrasing. In both of these cases, you are "borrowing" another author's ideas and/or words.

- If you find material you think you might use as a direct quotation in your research paper, be sure to *copy the information exactly*. One sign of a sloppy researcher is material that has been quoted incorrectly, for example, with spelling or grammatical errors. Use quotation marks in your notes to differentiate between material that is quoted and material that is paraphrased.

- *Jot down any critique, comments, or questions* that you have about the source that you have referenced. Notes like "Best source for information on demographics" or "Be sure to include chart—important economic data" could be invaluable when you sit down later to start writing your paper.

- You may also want to try *cross-referencing your notes with your paper outline* (see the following section on outlining). Imagine you find information in a source that refers to the section II. A. 4. in your outline. Put "II. A. 4." at the top of your note card or page. If you are concerned that the structure of your outline may change somewhat over time, you can also reference sections by name, such as "Presentation of Cases: Issue of Cost, Proponent Argument." Later when you begin to write your paper, pull all the cards that refer to each section of your outline. Using this method, the rough draft of your research paper emerges from the notes.

Here is an example of notes on an article researched for the Capstone topic, *Should Health Care Workers Be Tested for HIV/AIDS?*

Author: Dennis L. Breo
Title: "The Dental AIDS Cases—Murder or an Unsolvable Mystery?"
Publication: <u>Journal of the American Medical Association</u>, Vol. 270, No. 22, pages 2732–2734
Date: 8 Dec. 1993

Discusses the mystery of the Acer case. Dr. David Acer infected six of his dental patients with the AIDS virus. Three scenarios, given by Harald Jaffe, epidemiologist with the Center for Disease Control and Prevention):

　1 - accidental contamination of instruments, etc.

　2 - accidental personal injury, leading to infection of patients

　3 - murder/ motive was anger that he had been infected?

Details of the Bergalis case (infected patient). She came forward in October, 1990; filed suit against Acer's estate and dental insurer; died in 1991.
This led to Congress considering mandatory testing. Rejected. Compromise was voluntary precautions by health care workers.

　* Very good article on background of Acer case.

　* What was the result of Bergalis' suit? Other cases/suits re: Acer? Check it out.

- The note taker includes all the pertinent bibliographic material.
- The article is summarized in the author's own words and style.
- The writer includes comments and ideas for further research.

Outlining

Learning how to construct a successful outline is an important skill for any writer. Some instructors may require you to create an outline for your research paper. Even if your instructor does not do so, you should construct and use a comprehensive outline. Combined with thorough notes, a good outline will not only improve the quality of your research paper but also will make the task of writing it easier.

One advantage you have in writing your Capstone paper is the specific guidelines. These are detailed in the initial chapters of this handbook. The main points of those guidelines will assist you in formulating the outline for your paper. Review those chapters. Then read the following tips and example.

- Start with a clear thesis sentence or research question. In the Capstone project this will be your paper's central normative question.

- Construct the main headings of your outline so that they refer to the major sections required for the Capstone paper. Refer to the sample Capstone paper outline later in this section for a suggestion of what these sections will be.

- Create subheadings under each main heading to indicate how these main topics will be divided into smaller and then even smaller sections that directly relate to the content of your project.

- Make sure your outline flows in a logical order. Use a clear organizational scheme, such as by topic or chronology that will be apparent and easy to understand for your reader.

- Take the time to write a detailed outline.

- Realize that you will probably have to revise your outline more than once as you research your topic.

- Cross-reference your outline to your notes.

- Use your outline to help you discard any irrelevant, illogical, and redundant material.

Here is an example of a portion of a typical student's Capstone paper outline. It begins midway in the outline, as the student presents the cases.

Research Question: Should all health care workers be tested for HIV/AIDS?

II. Supporters' case
   A. Position: supporters argue all health care workers should be tested yearly.
      1. Specifics of how this policy would be carried out
      2. Details of how it would be funded

B. Supporters' parties to the controversy
   1. General supporters
      a. Almost all patients
         (1) Study done by the Apex Hospital Association in Florida
      b. Most insurance companies
      c. Half of all lawyers whose practices involve health care supporters
      d. [Continue with other general supporters]
   2. Leaders on the supporting side
      a. Robert Montgomery (Kimberly Bergalis' lawyer)
      b. Dr. David Lewis, University of Athens, GA
      c. [Continue with other leaders]
C. Supporters' arguments and the issues they address
   1. Issue of safety
      a. Argument: Medical and dental procedures are not completely safe.
         (1) Dr. David Lewis' research on dental instruments
         (2) Study done by University of CO re: laboratory procedures
         (3) Harold Jaffee (Center for Disease Control) re: hepatitis
      b. Argument: All patients have the right to be safe.
         (1) Discussion of the Hippocratic Oath by Dr. Rhonda Laterno, Baltimore Health Center
         (2) Kimberly Bergalis case
         (3) [Other supporting evidence regarding this argument]
   2. Issue of cost . . .

QUALITIES TO LOOK FOR IN YOUR OUTLINE:

Is the information logically developed, moving smoothly from point to point?

Does your paper follow a clear organizational scheme?

Does the information get more specific under each major heading?

Finally, remember that an essential part of the organization process is drafting and revision. You should create several drafts for *each* stage of your Capstone paper. Some writers will compose the whole paper, then go back and start a second draft. Others will compose one section, work on it until it seems fairly satisfactory, and then go on to the next. Either technique is acceptable, as long as you realize that *multiple drafts are required*. Remember to keep in mind that any work you do may require you to go back and adjust your outline according to new insights you have gained.

Generic Outline of a Capstone Paper

The following outline contains the elements usually included in a Capstone paper; it is, however, just a suggestion. Your instructor may require a slightly different format.

I. Introduction
   A. "Attention getter" and opening paragraph(s) ending with the research question
   B. Documentation of the social problem(s), including relevant statistics

    C. Definitions

    D. Scope

II. Development

    A. Background of the controversy

    B. Presentation of proponents' case

       1. Basic position on the case

       2. Parties holding the position

          a. General

          b. Specific

       3. Issues in contention

       4. Arguments with supporting evidence

       5. Proposed plans

       6. Main values

    C. Presentation of opponents' case

       1. Basic position on the case

       2. Parties holding the position

          a. General

          b. Specific

       3. Issues in contention

       4. Arguments with supporting evidence

       5. Proposed plans

       6. Main values

III. Analysis and Evaluation

    A. Analysis and evaluation of proponents' arguments and evidence

       1. Discussion of proponents' evidence

       2. Discussion of proponents' logic

    B. Analysis and evaluation of opponents' arguments and evidence

       1. Discussion of opponents' evidence

       2. Discussion of opponents' logic

    C. Analysis and evaluation of proponents' moral reasoning

       1. Obligations

       2. Values

       3. Consequences

       4. Normative Principles

    D. Analysis and evaluation of opponents' moral reasoning

       1. Obligations

       2. Values

       3. Consequences

       4. Normative principles

    E. Tentative Solution

       1. Discussion of author's tentative solution

          a. Arguments (preliminary)

b. Moral reasoning (preliminary)

c. Practical plan or policy

2. OPTIONAL: Discussion of civic engagement activity (if activity is not included here, it should appear in section IV)

IV. Experiential Component and Revised Solution

A. Discussion of expert interviews

1. Introduction of the interviewees

2. Presentation of interviewees' responses

3. Analysis of interviews

B. OPTIONAL: Discussion of civic engagement activity (if activity is not included here, it should appear in III.E.2.)

C. Revised solution

1. Author's arguments (revised)

2. Author's moral reasoning (revised)

3. Presentation of and response to major counterarguments

4. Author's plan or policy (revised)

5. Final thoughts

Style

Style is sometimes referred to as "the writer's voice." An outstanding research paper needs to be complete in terms of content, well organized, and accurate in terms of grammar, spelling, and punctuation. However, it also must be interesting and appropriate in terms of word choice, phrasing, and sentence variety. The following are guidelines to help you achieve a voice appropriate to the Capstone paper.

Your Capstone paper is a formal research paper written for an academic audience. As such, it is a form of writing that requires you to gather facts, information, and other materials about your topic from outside sources and to use some type of standardized documentation of those sources. In this way it resembles the type of reference writing with which most of you are familiar, the report. In report writing you gather information from outside sources and explain the idea to an audience in the clearest manner possible. The rhetorical intent is *to inform*. Usually the report writer makes no explicit judgment or interpretation of the information collected. The writer's personal imprint is made only in the presentation of the facts. While your Capstone paper contains elements of the report, as a research paper it will also require you to use additional skills.

While the first portion of the Capstone paper, in which you present the background of the controversy and the details of each side's cases, requires you to maintain the objective tone of the report, later sections require you to take a stand on the controversy. In the sections of your paper you write for Submissions Three and Four, you must present your own critical judgment on the controversy, based on a detailed examination and analysis of outside sources. Unlike the report, this section of your research paper requires you to make a judgment or interpretation of the facts and information presented. While such a paper shares the report's rhetorical goal to inform, it additionally requires the author *to analyze* and *to persuade*.

The following suggestions will help you to maintain the formal tone required by the Capstone paper. They will also help you to successfully inform your reader about the controversy you have chosen to investigate; analyze the arguments, evidence, and moral reasoning of the various parties involved in the debate; and persuade your reader to support what you determine to be the best solution to the social controversy.

- Use the appropriate tone. It should be *formal,* rather than informal; businesslike, rather than creative; scholarly rather than conversational.
  - Imagine yourself reading your paper to a group like the City Council. Would your work be appropriate?
- Do not use any contractions or slang. They lend a flavor of informality.
  - Laws are enforced by police, not "cops."
  - A good argument is impressive, not "awesome."
  - Young people are children, not "kids."
- Work for *precision* in your writing.
  - Consider which sentence gives the reader better, more accurate information?

    Patients are in favor of testing heath care workers for HIV/AIDS.

    or

    Most patients are in favor of testing health care workers for HIV/AIDS, according to a survey taken of 3,000 patients by the Americus hospital system, based in California (Donelson 33).
- Be *concise* in your writing. Say what you need to say with precision, and avoid rambling repetitive writing.
  - Try reading portions of your paper out loud—your ear will catch wordiness that your eye misses. Read your paper with the idea that every extra word would cost you $1.00!
- Write with *your own voice.* Do not fall into the trap of writing a paper that is a string of other writers' direct quotations. Quote selectively and paraphrase frequently (but remember to give credit through parenthetical citations after the material you have used).
  - There are just a few reasons to use direct quotations. Use them only when conveying complicated language and ideas that need to be expressed exactly or when the authors' words are so powerful that you could not say it any better.
- Be sensitive to the social connotations in language. These involve areas such as gender, religion, sexual orientation, and race.
  - If you are referring to a person who could be a man or a woman, do not use "he." To avoid this, try making the noun plural if possible (for example, change "person" to "people") so that you can then use the gender-neutral pronoun, "they." Otherwise, you should say "he or she."
  - The following are terms generally used to refer to identify particular groups by religion, sexual orientation, and race. If you are using a term to refer to these groups that is not included in this list and are unsure of its connotations, you should check with your instructor.

    Common religious groups: Christians, Jews, Muslims, Buddhists, Hindus

    Common sexual orientations: heterosexual, homosexual (gay, lesbian), bisexual

    Common terms referencing a person by his or her race: African American, Black, Latino, Hispanic, Asian, American Indian, Arab, White.

    Be sure to correctly apply terms that reference nationality. For example, the terms *Japanese American, Irish American,* and *Mexican American* all refer to a person who holds citizenship in the United States but who may have been born in another country or whose ancestors were from that country. The terms *Japanese, Irish,* and *Mexican* refer to people who are citizens of another country and who do not hold U.S. citizenship.
- Proofread your work. You lose all credibility as a writer if your research paper contains typos and small errors that could be easily fixed with a thorough proofing.

- Consider what would you think of a textbook that told you this: "The American Revolvolution was frought in the late 1900s between the potriots and the solderers of the Kling of Kengland."

Grammar, Spelling, and Punctuation

You are living in the computer age. This technology can work for you when you write a research paper. Take the time to USE GRAMMAR AND SPELL-CHECK!

However, technology cannot do all the work. These computer aids *do not* replace actual proofreading of your writing. You need to have a command of at least the basics of grammar, spelling, and punctuation. If you do not, you cannot communicate your thoughts clearly to your readers. You do not want mechanical errors to get in the way of the content of your writing. The following are tips about problem areas that writers often need to tackle. But remember, if you need more help on the mechanics of writing, it is out there. Seek help from your instructor, the Writing Center, Academic Planning and Support Services, and grammar handbooks.

- Use a dictionary to help you spell.
- Watch for words that are often confused due to sounding alike or similar spellings. For example:
  - affect and effect
  - through, though, and thought
  - quiet and quite
  - counsel and council
  - its and it's
  - your and you're
  - their and there
  - to, too, and two
  - pair and pear
  - capital and capitol
  - whose and who's
  - principal and principle
- Be sure that the subject and verb of your sentences agree. Both need to be the same, either singular or plural.

"The general orders an attack on the opposing army."

NOT

"The general order an attack on the opposing army."

- Be sure that the nouns and corresponding pronouns that you use agree. This error is common for writers attempting to use gender-neutral pronouns. It can often be corrected by making the noun plural.

"Patients should know their rights."

OR

"A patient should know his or her rights."

NOT

"A patient should know their rights."

- Be sure that the tense of your work—past, present, or future—is correct and consistent.

  "The treaty was signed in 1914. The fighting stopped immediately."

  NOT

  "The treaty was signed in 1914. The fighting will stop immediately."

- Learn what punctuation is appropriate in each situation. This includes periods, commas, semicolons, colons, dashes, and exclamation points.

  - For example, did you know that you use a semicolon in a sentence like this one, "The legislation was discussed; however, no consensus was reached," because the main clauses are closely related?

- Be sure that in all titles, including the title of your research paper and those of the works you cite, the first letter of every word is capitalized, except

  - Articles, like *a, an,* and *the*
  - Prepositions, like *in, of,* and *to*
  - Conjunctions, like *and, or,* and *but*
  - The *to* in an infinitive, like *to Read*

- Capitalize if you are referring to the specific title of something; do not capitalize if you are referring to something generally.

  "George Bush, the President of the United States, spoke to the press."

  versus

  "Several presidents of small universities were at the meeting."

NEED MORE INFORMATION?

The <u>MLA Handbook</u> covers almost everything you need to know about the mechanics of writing. Don't guess. Refer to it!

Online Resources for Help with Writing

Information on Grammar, Punctuation, and Style

OWL: The Online Writing Lab at Purdue University
   http://owl.english.purdue.edu/owl/

Writing Resources—Princeton University Writing Center
   http://web.princeton.edu/sites/writing/Writing_Center/WCWritingRes.htm

LEO: Literacy Education Online—The Write Place at St. Cloud University
   http://leo.stcloudstate.edu/

Writing Resources for Students—Doyle Online Writing Lab, Reed College
   http://academic.reed.edu/writing/

The Elements of Style by William Strunk, Jr.—Online book at Bartleby.com
   http://www.bartleby.com/141/

English as a Second Language

ESL Resources, Handouts, and Exercises—The Online Writing Lab at Purdue University
    http://owl.english.purdue.edu/handouts/esl/index.html

Self-Study Questions for ESL Students—*The Internet TESL Journal*
    http://a4esl.org/q/h/

English as a Second Language—Rong-Chang Li, Ph.D.
    http://www.rong-chang.com/

Help Tackling a Large Research Paper

Writing a Thesis—Writing Program at Dartmouth College
    http://www.dartmouth.edu/%7Ewriting/materials/student/thesis.shtml

Research Papers—Jim Moore, Ph.D., Associate Professor of Anthropology at University of California, San Diego
    http://weber.ucsd.edu/~jmoore/courses/researchpapers.html

MLA Format

Writers of scholarly manuscripts such as a Capstone paper follow guidelines that detail the mechanics of how the document should be written. There are several different styles; however, Capstone uses the guidelines in the *MLA Handbook for Writers of Research Papers*. One of the requirements of this project is that you write according to MLA specifications. Most instructors require you to purchase the *MLA Handbook* for this course. The information in this section is designed to give you an overview of the most commonly used sections of the handbook, but it cannot replace the *Handbook*.

MLA Style Basics

Title Page

MLA does not call for a separate title page. Instead, pertinent information is written on the first page of the paper. Include your name and/or ID number, your professor's name, the course name and section, and the date the paper is submitted in the upper left corner; this is the paper's "Heading." For purposes of anonymity in cross-sectional grading and the Capstone Paper of the Year Competition, for Submission Five you should replace your name in the upper left hand corner and the header with your student ID number. Omit your professor's name and include only your section number.

Margins

For the top margin of the paper, use one (1) inch. You also must include your last name and the page number flush with the right margin, one-half (1/2) inch from the top of the page in the paper's "Header" (this is the "header's" default margin in the *Normal* document template in Microsoft *Word*). Also use a 1-inch margin for the right, left, and bottom margins. *CAUTION:* The default left and right margins for the *Word Normal* template is 1.25 inches; you should change these margin settings immediately on beginning your paper's word processing to avoid future formatting problems.

Page Numbering

Page numbering begins with the first page of the paper with continuous sequential numbers *to include* any appendices and the Works Cited. In the page numbering Header, your last name should appear first with *one* space separating it from the page number (i.e., Smith 1). As noted above, this will be changed to your ID number for Submission Five (i.e., 76000 1).

Spacing

All text is double-spaced in the paper, even block quotes and the Works Cited entries.

Quotations and Attributive Tags

Attributive tags are phrases used to integrate quotations into the rest of a paragraph. They may appear before, after, or between quoted material. The following examples present each of these formats:

In her article, "Bioethics," Madeline Shelton explains, "Biologists today are increasingly aware of the ethical ramifications of their work" (22).

"Biologists today," *explains Madeline Shelton in her article,* "Bioethics," "are increasingly aware of the ethical ramifications of their work" (22).

"Biologists today are increasingly aware of the ethical ramifications of their work," *explains Madeline Shelton in her article,* "Bioethics" (22).

Use attributive tags consistently in both short and long quotations as transitions to connect your thoughts to the concepts expressed in a quotation. They are also important in clarifying the origin of the quoted material and establishing the original author's credibility. In these attributions, you should give your reader an idea of *why* the words of the person you quote are important. What are his or her credentials? You may want to list an author's position or title ("CEO of Walmart," "professor of history at Columbia University," "chief of pediatric surgery at the Mayo Clinic") or indicate his or her accomplishments relevant to the subject matter at hand ("Nobel Prize winner," "author of Stem Cell Research and the Future," "former prisoner of war"). When you use an author's name for the first time in your paper, be sure to give his or her first and last name. On subsequent references, the last name alone is sufficient.

Short Quotations

Short quotations, those four lines and shorter (in your text), are included as part of the paper's text and are punctuated as follows: ". . . of the twentieth century" (Rubens 23). Notice that the terminating punctuation goes outside the closing parentheses of the parenthetical documentation if the quote ends with a period; if the quoted sentence ends with some other form of terminal punctuation, i.e., ? or !, that mark goes *inside* the quotation marks with a period still following the closing parentheses [". . . of the twentieth century?" (Rubens 23).]. If your quote does not end with a terminal punctuation, then you *MUST* include an ellipsis [. . .] between the last letter of the last word and the closing quotation marks, to show that it is an incomplete sentence.

Long Quotations

Quotations of more than four typed lines (in your text) should be presented as a double-spaced block quote of text indented one inch from the left page margin and even with the right page margin. Quotation marks are not used around the quotation. Parenthetical documentation showing the quotation's source must also be provided. Unlike the short quotation format, with a block quote the terminal punctuation is placed in its usual place at the end of the sentence, followed by a space and then the parenthetical citation. (See the MLA Handbook for rules on paragraph indents and quotations within block quotes.)

Use of the First Person Singular

Some instructors discourage the use of "I" ("I reviewed the research . . ."), preferring a passive voice or similar construction ("A review of the research was done . . ."). But many modern writers of research reports use "I" to express their opinions and conclusions and find that preferable to constructions such as "this writer." Your instructor will give you specific instructions.

Documentation or Citation

In writing your paper, you must document everything you use from an outside source. The MLA style requires two types of documentation. First, parenthetical documentations are inserted in your paper wherever you incorporate another's words or ideas. Second, a list of sources, or Works Cited, is included at the end of the paper.

Parenthetical Documentation

Immediately after the outside material included the paper's text, a parenthetical documentation pointing to the source's entry on the Works Cited should be included. The last name of the author of the included material and the page(s) on which it is found are normally all that is required, as in (Smith 33). For other types of entries (multiple works by the same author, works without named authors, etc.), see the appropriate section of the MLA Handbook.

Works Cited

Your Works Cited will begin on a new page following the last page of text (including appendices) of your paper, but the Works Cited List will be numbered as a part of the paper's continuous pagination. The Works Cited should include only the sources actually cited in the text of your paper. The title Works Cited (*not* "Bibliography" or "References") should appear centered at the top of your list of entries, and all works used in the paper should be listed in alphabetical order, regardless of whether the entry is an author's last name or a source title. All text in your Work Cited—even if an entry is longer than one line—should be double-spaced. If you use a work that has no author or editor, it should be alphabetized according to the title, ignoring any article such as *A, An,* or *The.* (The Chicago Manual of Style would be alphabetized under C.)

Samples of Citation Forms

The following list gives examples of some of the most commonly used citation forms. *The entry form is shown first, followed by the appropriate parenthetical documentation form.* [Refer to The MLA Handbook for Writers of Research Papers Chapter 7 for authorized abbreviations.]

Books by a single author

Gershman, Herbert S. The Surrealist Revolution in France. Ann Arbor: U of Michigan P, 1969.
(Gershman 246)

Books by two or three authors

Eggins, Suzanne, and Diana Slade. Analysing Casual Conversation. London: Cassell, 1997.
(Eggins and Slade 212)

Raffer, Bernard C., Richard Friedman, and Robert Baron. New York Crisis. New York: Harper, 1971.
(Raffer, Friedman, and Baron 246)

Books by four or more authors

Gilman, Sander, Helen King, Roy Porter, and George Rousseau. Hysteria beyond Freud.
    Berkeley: U of California P, 1993.

Gilman, Sander, et al. Hysteria beyond Freud Berkeley: U of California P, 1993.
(Gilman et al. 143)

Note: If the number of authors exceeds five or six, the "et al." form should be used in the Works Cited entry as well as in the parenthetical documentation.

Two or more books by the same author

Durant, Will. The Age of Faith. New York: Simon, 1950. Vol. 4 of The Story of Civilization. 11
    vols. 1935–75.

———. Our Oriental Heritage. New York: Simon, 1951. Vol. 6 of The Story of Civilization.
    11 vols. 1935–75.

(Durant, Age of Faith 334) and (Durant, Our Oriental 278)

A book with an editor instead of an author

Hawkes, Jacquetta, ed. <u>The World of the Past</u>. New York: Knopf, 1963.

(Hawkes 254)

Article in a journal that pages each issue separately

Brogdon, Robert. "Religious Freedom and School Holidays." <u>Journal of Communication</u> 50.4
    (1995): 90–110.

(Brogdon 99)

An article in a journal with continuous pagination

Spear, Karen. "Building Skills in Basic Writing." <u>Teaching English in the Two-Year College</u> 9
    (1995): 391–99.

(Spear 397)

Authored article in a magazine or newspaper

Baron, Caroline. "Southern Africa: Trade Feeds on Independence." <u>Business Week</u> 14 Feb. 1987:
    66–67.

(Baron 66)

Article without a named author in a magazine or newspaper

"Unrest Widespread in Cuba." <u>New York Times</u> 9 Apr. 1996: 15, 31.

("Unrest" 15)

Article from a daily newspaper

Collins, Greg. "Single-Father Survey Finds Adjustment a Problem." <u>New York Times</u> 21 Nov.
    1986, late ed.: B17.

(Collins) [Page number is NOT required if it is a single page article.]

An article from a weekly or biweekly periodical

Begley, Sharon. "Our Mother Earth." <u>Newsweek</u> 4 Nov. 1991: 45–47.

(Begley 46)

An article from a monthly or bimonthly periodical

Snyder, Mark. "Self-Fulfilling Stereotypes." <u>Psychology Today</u> July 1988: 60–70.

(Snyder 65–67)

Authored encyclopedia article

Rogers, Robert. "The Arctic Circle." <u>Encyclopedia Americana</u>. 1996 ed.

(Rogers 1068)

Encyclopedia article without a named author

"Color and Light." <u>Encyclopedia Americana</u>. 1994 ed.

("Color" 1204)

Government publications

United States. Dept. of State. <u>The Cambodian Situation</u> 1971. Washington: GPO, 1977.

(US Dept. of State 145)

Note: Most federal publications are published by the Government Printing Office (GPO).

Bible

<u>The New Jerusalem Bible</u>. Henry Wansbrough, gen. ed. New York: Doubleday, 1985.

(<u>New Jerusalem Bible</u>, Ezek. 1.5–10)

Interviews

Masters, James. Personal interview. 30 June 2007.

Rogers, Sally. Telephone interview. 6 Aug. 2007.

(Masters) and (Rogers)

NOTE

Citation of electronic publications is an area that is constantly evolving with technology. The following citations are examples only. You should use the current edition of the <u>MLA Handbook</u> and carefully refer to relevant section as you cite electronic publications in your paper.

Online databases or subscription services

Generally, entries for material from online databases requires you to first provide the required information for the print version and then follow with information specific to the fact that you have accessed the material from an online database or subscription service. The following information is required:

Author's last name, first name. "Title of the article." <u>Title of the journal</u> vol. number.issue

number (year of publication): page number(s). <u>Name of the database</u>. Name of the computer

service. Library, City. Date of access.

Please note that you are no longer required to provide the URL of computer service's home page.

McGowan, Alan H. "Renewable Energy Now." <u>Environment</u> 48.6 (2006): 1. <u>Academic Search</u>

<u>Premier</u>. EBSCO Host. Scarborough-Phillips Lib., Austin. 10 July 2006.

(McGowan 1)

Zink, Samantha. "The Equal Rights Amendment." <u>Legal Issues</u> 13.4 (1995): 103–19.

<u>Congressional Universe</u>. Lexis-Nexis. Scarborough-Phillips Lib., Austin. 12 Nov. 2001.

(Zink 110)

NOTE

Congressional Quarterly has various publications (<u>CQ Weekly</u>; <u>The CQ Researcher</u>) and collections (Public Affairs Collection; Supreme Court Collection) both in print and on multiple databases. All of the databases are currently resident in the CQ Electronic Library Subscription Service. See your instructor or a Scarborough-Phillips Library reference librarian for further guidance on the proper entry forms for each publication and database.

NOTE

Page numbers should be provided ONLY if document is in .pdf format; page numbers from html documents are NOT usable for citation purposes.

World Wide Web pages

When citing a Web page the following information is required:

Name of the person who authored the material on the Web site (if known). <u>Title of Web site</u>. Date of publication or last revision. Name of institution or organization associated with the site. Date of access <URL>.

Often, however, these Web sites may not supply all desired information. In these cases, the researcher must settle for whatever information is available:

"Al Gore's Justice Department Says Second Amendment Is Meaningless." <u>NRA-ILA Research & Information Web site</u> 25 Sept. 1999. National Rifle Association. 3 Feb. 2007 <http://www.nraila.org/990925.html>.

("Al Gore's Justice")

Biggs, Andrew G. "The Archer-Shaw Social Security Plan: Laying the Groundwork for Another S&L Crisis—Executive Summary." <u>Cato Institute Briefing Papers</u> (No. 55) 16 Apr. 2000. Cato Institute Web site. 3 Feb. 2007 <http://www.cato.org/pubs/briefs/bp-055es.html>.

(Biggs)

"The Case for Public Access to Federally Funded Research Data." <u>Cato Policy Analysis</u> (No. 366) 2 June 2000. Cato Institute Web site. 3 Feb. 2007 <http://www.cato.org/pubs/pas/pa-366es.pdf>.

("Case for" 46)

<u>Cato Institute Home Page</u>. 3 Feb. 2007 <http://www.cato.org/home.html>.

(Cato)

<u>Dallas Business Opportunities Web site</u>. 31 Dec. 2001. Dallas Coalition for Economic Growth. 4 Jan. 2007 <http://www.dallco.org/ business/2001>.

(Dallas)

Online Book

Austen, Jane. <u>Pride and Prejudice</u>. Ed. Henry Churchyard. 1996. <u>Jane Austen Information Page</u>. 6 Sept. 2002 <http://www.pemberley.com/janeinfo/pridprej.html>.

Emerson, Ralph Waldo. <u>Essays: First Series</u>. 1841. 12 Feb. 1997 <ftp://ftp.books.com/ebooks/NonFiction/Philosophy/Emerson/history/txt>.

Nagata, Linda. Goddesses. 2000. Scifi.com. 2002. 4 Oct. 2002 <http://www.scifi.com/originals/originals_archive/nagata/>.

NOTE

Your instructor is the "final authority" on conformation to <u>MLA Handbook</u> style and completeness of Works Cited entries.

Quick Guide for Formatting Papers

- Typed, 12-point *maximum;* 11-point *minimum* in a "standard" font (e.g., Times Roman, Arial, Courier)

- *Double-spacing* throughout entire paper

- One (1) inch margins: top and bottom of pages; left and right sides of pages

- First page, upper left contains [*double-spaced*]:

  Your Name
  Instructor's Name
  Course Name & Number (including Section #)
  Date (MLA format: 8 Dec. 2007)

- Title, centered above text, on first page (do not put in quotation marks, bold, italics, or underline)

- Each page is numbered in upper right corner, preceded by your last name (changed to your ID number for Submission Five)

- Securely fastened together with staples or large-sized binder clips

- Proofed for obvious typographical, spelling, grammar, and other errors

---

NOTE

Refer to the page titled First Page of a Research Paper in the sample pages of the <u>MLA Handbook</u>.

Quick Guide for Quotations

When you copy any text exactly from another author's work, you need to use a specific format to indicate to your readers what you have done. While all quotations should use attributive tags as indicated here, the two types of quotations—short and long—are formatted differently.

All Quotations

- All quotations should be introduced with attributive tags, transitional phrases connecting your thoughts with the quoted material. Generally attributive tags should identify the source of the quotation and establish his or her credibility (see the following).

  Dr. Leon Chisholm, Director of the Institute for Deep-Sea Research, calls this innovation "the most important development of the twentieth century" (220).

Short Quotations

- These are quotations four typed lines and shorter in your text.
- They are included as part of the text, set off with quotation marks.
- If a parenthetical citation (see the following) follows the quotation, the punctuation—period, comma, or anything else—goes outside the closing parenthesis.

  The art critic Shaw writes, "Nowhere can you find the depth of feeling and the riot of color and shape that are present in contemporary Mexican art" (113).

Long (Block) Quotations

- These are quotations of more than four typed lines in your text.
- The text is indented one inch from the left margin (twice the standard paragraph indent).
- The text on the right maintains the normal one-inch margin.
- As with the rest of the research paper, every line is double-spaced.
- Quotation marks are not used—the indentation takes their place.
- A colon is normally used after the text, before the quotation.
- The parenthetical citation is placed *after* the punctuation (see the following).

  Professor Sanders, who has studied in Afghanistan, contends that a land war in the country will be fruitless:

  > **The terrain is extremely mountainous. Think of the pictures of the moon that have come back from space. In addition, there are caves everywhere, and the Afghani people are acclimated to surviving in them if the need arises. Then the weather is impossible. Once the winter begins in October, any kind of attack will be impossible. In short, I would predict Vietnam all over again, just in a colder climate. (114)**

REMEMBER

The punctuation goes *after the closing parentheses* in short quotations and *after the text* in blocked quotations.

Quick Guide for Documentation of Sources

As mentioned earlier, one important aspect of your research paper is appropriately giving credit to the sources you have used in your work. You need to do this in two ways:

- Short parenthetical documentation in the body of the paper
- Complete bibliographic documentation, a Works Cited, at the end of the paper

Parenthetical Documentation

As you are writing your research paper, it is important that you indicate to the reader what works you are using and where in that work you found the material. You do this by adding a short parenthetical acknowledgement in your paper whenever you incorporate another's words or ideas.

- Usually the author's last name and a page number are sufficient:

One theory is that President Reagan purposely chose to ignore the AIDS epidemic in the early 1980s, hoping that there would be a quick resolution without the federal government having to get involved (Del vecchio 120).

- If the author's name appears in your text, cite the appropriate page number only:

Del vecchio's theory is that President Reagan purposely ignored the AIDS situation, hoping that the federal government would not need to get involved. He believed that the epidemic would be limited to the homosexual community and would be quickly resolved (120).

- If you are using more than one book or article by the same author, include the author's last name, a shortened version of the appropriate title and a page number:

President Reagan has been criticized for ignoring the AIDS epidemic in the early 1980s. It is possible that he underestimated the seriousness of the situation and believed there would be a quick resolution (Del vecchio, "The AIDS Crisis" 120).

Documented in Works Cited as:

Del vecchio, Samson. "The AIDS Crisis and Where We Are Now." Journal of Modern Political Thought 19 (1999) 714–24. Expanded Academic ASAP. InfoTrac. Scarborough-Phillips Lib., Austin. 30 Dec. 2000.

- If there is no author, cite a shortened version of the title as it appears in the Works Cited:

In September 1985, President Reagan held a press conference to discuss the Ryan White situation. He indicated that he could understand why parents would not want their children to go to school with students, like White, who have AIDS ("President Responds" 12).

Documented in Works Cited as:

"President Responds to the AIDS Crisis." New York Times. 8 Oct 1985, late ed.: A15.

- Remember that the parenthetical documentation must follow the format of the bibliographic documentation in the Works Cited, so that the reader can find the complete documentation easily:

A study published in The American Family predicted the growth of single-parent homes in the United States (National Research Council 311).

Documented in Works Cited as:

National Research Council. The American Family. Washington: Natl. Acad. 1995.

- Remember, you must include parenthetical documentation *whether you borrow another's exact words (a direct quote) or his or her ideas (paraphrasing).* Failure to give credit in either case is plagiarism, or cheating. (See the chapter titled "Academic Honesty" for more information.)

NOTE

The preceding are examples only. You need to consult the <u>MLA Handbook</u> for information about citing specific research materials.

Quick Guide for Works Cited List

(see "First Page of Works Cited" in the sample pages of your <u>MLA Handbook</u>)

- Put your sources on separate page(s) after the text and appendices. These pages will have the same header and continuous pagination with the rest of the Capstone paper.
- The title, Works Cited, should be centered at the top of the page.
- Put *only* the sources you have cited in the text on this page. That is, if there is no parenthetical citation for a source within your text, it should not be listed on the "Works Cited" list.
- Arrange the sources you have used in alphabetical order.

WHAT DO I DO IF THERE'S NO AUTHOR?

If a source has no author, alphabetize it according to the first word, usually the title, ignoring articles (*A*, *An*, and *The*).

- *Double-space everything.*
- If the citation runs to two lines or more, indent the second, third, fourth, etc., line five spaces (hanging indent). See examples in the previous sections of this chapter.
- Each citation should exactly follow MLA format.
- Proofread carefully for typos and other errors.

NOTE

You should purchase the most recent edition of the <u>MLA Handbook</u>. It is available in the university bookstore.

Works Cited (Example)

American Cancer Society. "Tobacco and Cancer." 2006. 15 July 2006.

<http://www.cancer.orgdownloads/PRO/Tobacco.pdf>.

Fieser, James. "Ethics." <u>The Internet Encyclopedia of Philosophy</u>. Eds. James Fieser and Bradley

Dowden. The U of Tennessee at Martin. 5 Sept. 2006.

<http://www.iep.utm.edu/e/ethics/htm>.

"Metropolitan Survey Finds Strong Public Support for MH Parity." <u>Mental Health Weekly</u> 14 (2004):

1–3. <u>Academic Search Premier</u>. EBSCOHost. Scarborough-Phillips Lib., Austin. 20 Feb. 2006.

Ruggiero, Vincent Ryan. <u>Thinking Critically about Ethical Issues</u>. 6th ed. New York:

McGraw-Hill, 2004.

"Should the Draft Be Reinstated?" <u>Time</u> 29 Dec. 2003: 101–02.